Gender and Teaching

REFLECTIVE TEACHING
AND THE SOCIAL CONDITIONS OF SCHOOLING
A Series for Prospective and Practicing Teachers
Daniel P. Liston and Kenneth M. Zeichner, Series Editors

Gender and Teaching

Frances A. Maher
Wheaton College

Janie Victoria Ward
Simmons College

 LAWRENCE ERLBAUM ASSOCIATES, PUBLISHERS
2002   Mahwah, New Jersey   London

#4584624

Lawrence Erlbaum Associates, Inc., Publishers
10 Industrial Avenue
Mahwah, New Jersey 07430

Cover design by Kathryn Houghtaling Lacey

Library of Congress Cataloging-in-Publication Data

Maher, Frances A.
  Gender and teaching / Frances A. Maher, Janie V. Ward.
    p. cm. — (Reflective teaching and the social conditions of schooling)
  Includes bibliographical references and index.
  ISBN 0-8058-2986-5 (pbk. : alk. paper)
1. Sex differences in education–United States–Case studies.
2. Teaching–Social aspects–United States–Case studies. 3. Educational
equalization–United States–Case studies. I. Ward, Janie Victoria.
II. Title. III. Series.
  LC212.92 .M34 2002
  306.43 – dc21
                                                    00-023133
                                                    CIP

Books published by Lawrence Erlbaum Associates are printed on acid-free paper,
and their bindings are chosen for strength and durability.

Printed in the United States of America
10 9 8 7 6 5 4 3 2

CONTENTS

II. PUBLIC ARGUMENTS   73

III. FINAL ARGUMENTS, AND SOME
SUGGESTIONS AND RESOURCES
FOR FURTHER REFLECTION   109

SERIES PREFACE

AN ESSENTIAL SERIES INTRODUCTION

Whereas many readers rarely read introductory material, we hope you will continue. The success of this book depends, in large part, on how you use it. In what follows we outline some of our key assumptions and we suggest ways for approaching the material in each book of this series entitled, "Reflective Teaching and the Social Conditions of School." First we identify some of our reasons for creating this series. We then relate a bit about our dissatisfaction with how teacher education is usually conducted and how it can be changed. Finally we outline suggestions for ways to best utilize the material in this and subsequent texts.

A few years ago we were asked to develop further the ideas outlined in our book *Teacher Education and the Social Conditions of Schooling* (Liston & Zeichner, 1991). It was suggested that we take our basic approach to teacher reflection and our ideas about teacher education curricula and put them into practice. The proposal was attractive and the subsequent endeavor proved to be very challenging. It never seems easy to translate educational "shoulds" and possibilities into schooling "cans" and realities. But we think (and we hope) we have made progress in that effort by designing a series of books intended to help prospective, beginning, and experienced teachers to reflect on their profession, their teaching, and their experiences. We are pleased and delighted to have the opportunity to share this work with you. We hope you will find these texts to be engaging and useful.

We are two university teacher educators, both former elementary teachers, who have worked in inner-city, small town, and suburban elementary and middle schools. We are committed to public schools as democratic institutions, as places of learning in which people of all walks of life come to learn how to live together in a democratic society. Although we are personally committed to ways of working and living together that are much more collaborative than exist today—we are educators first, realists second, and dreamers third. It is our firm belief that an education that engages prospective and practicing teachers' heads and hearts, their beliefs and passions, needs to be fair and honest. We have neither written nor encouraged others to write these texts to convince you to see schools and society in a particular light, but rather to engage you in a consideration of crucial issues that all teachers need to address. Once engaged we hope that you will be better able to articulate your views, responses, and responsibilities to students and parents, and come to better understand aspects of your role as a teacher in a democratic society.

IMPACTS OF THE SOCIAL CONDITIONS OF SCHOOLING

Prospective teachers need to be prepared for the problems and challenges of public schooling. Sometimes the focus in schools (departments and colleges) of education remains strictly on the processes that occur within the classroom and inside the school walls. At times teacher education programs emphasize instructional methodology and the psychology of the learner in university course work and underscore survival strategies for student teaching. These are certainly important elements in any teacher's preparation and ones that cannot be ignored. But classrooms and schools are not insulated environments. What goes on inside schools is greatly influenced by what occurs outside of schools. The students who attend and the teachers and administrators who work within those walls bring into the school building all sorts of cultural assumptions, social influences, and contextual dynamics. Unless some concerted attention is given to those assumptions, influences, and dynamics, to the reality of school life and to the social conditions of schooling, our future teachers will be ill prepared. Over the last ten years, teacher educators have paid greater attention to the social conditions of schooling. But a consensus of opinion on this issue does not exist. Recently, the professional aspects of teacher education, including attention to the social conditions of schooling, have been criticized by scholars and politicians such as those associated with the Fordham Foundation who believe that content knowledge alone is sufficient to teach. This view, we believe, is a gross and politically motivated mistake that will do harm to the students in our public schools and their teachers. Students need teachers who have the professional preparation necessary to teach a greatly diverse student population to high academic standards. We hope that the books in this series will contribute to this end.

We are living in a time of remarkable change, a time of social and political transformation. In an era that promises to be rife with social controversies and political difficulties, in which public schooling will increasingly come under attack, during which we will see marked changes in this country's cultural demographic make-up, in which there will be great pressure to transform public schools into private-for-profit enterprises, our teaching workforce must be well prepared. Future teachers cannot, on their own, solve the many societal issues confronting the schools, but they should certainly know what those issues are, have a sense of their own beliefs about those issues, and understand the many ways in which those issues will come alive within their school's walls. Poverty and wealth, our culture of consumerism, what seems to be an increasing amount of violent behavior, and the work pressures of modern life affect the children who attend our public schools. Public attitudes about competition and excellence, race and ethnicity, gender roles and homosexuality, and the environment affect students inside and outside of schools. One can be certain that the issues that affect all of our lives outside of schools will certainly influence students inside their schools.

EXAMINING THE SOCIAL CONDITIONS OF SCHOOLING

Probably the best way to begin to examine contextual issues such as these is to be "attentive" early on in one's professional preparation, to experience features of the social conditions of schooling, and then to examine the experience and what we know about the social and cultural context of schooling. We encourage prospective and practicing teachers to do this. But teacher preparation programs often are not organized in a fashion that would encourage the discussion and examination of these sorts of shared experiences. What traditionally are called *social foundations* courses are typically not school-based, but set apart from some of the more realistic, practical, and engaged dilemmas of schooling. In schools of education we frequently teach what the sociology or philosophy of education has to say about schools but we tend to teach it as sociologists or philosophers, not as teachers struggling with crucial and highly controversial issues. Thus, in our own work with prospective and practicing teachers we have developed ways to examine contextual issues of schooling and to enable ourselves and students to articulate our ideas, beliefs, theories, and feelings about those issues. The books in this series attempt to utilize some of these insights and to pass along to others the content and the processes we have found useful.

When students and faculty engage in discussions of the social and political conditions of schooling and the effects of these conditions on students and schools, it is likely that the talk will be lively and controversies will emerge. In this arena there are no absolutely "right" or "wrong" answers. There are choices, frequently difficult ones, choices that require considerable discussion, deliberation, and justification. In order for these discussions to occur we need to create classroom settings that are conducive to conversations about difficult and controversial issues. The best format for such discussion is not the debate, the (in)formal argument, or dispassionate and aloof analysis. Instead the most conducive environment is a classroom designed to create dialogue and conversation among participants with differing points of view. There isn't a recipe or formula that will ensure this type of environment but we think the following suggestions are worth considering.

It is important for individuals using these texts to engage in discussions that are sensitive and respectful toward others, and at the same time challenge each other's views. This is not an easy task. It requires each participant to come to the class sessions prepared, to listen attentively to other people's views, and to address one another with a tone and attitude of respect. This means that when disagreements between individuals occur, and they inevitably will occur, each participant should find a way to express that disagreement without diminishing or attacking the other individual. Participants in these professional discussions need to be able to voice their views freely and to be sensitive toward others. Frequently, this is difficult to do. In discussions of controversial issues, ones that strike emotional chords, we are prone to argue in a way that belittles or disregards another person and their point of view. At times, we try to dismiss both the claim and the person. But if the discussions that these books help to initiate are carried on in that demeaning fashion,the potential power of

these works will not be realized. A discussion of this paragraph should occur before discussing the substance raised by this particular text. It is our
conviction that when a class keeps both substance and pedagogy in the
forefront it has a way of engaging individuals in a much more positive
manner. From our own past experiences we have found that during the
course of a class's use of this material it may be quite helpful to pause and
focus on substantive and pedagogical issues in a conscious and forthright
manner. Such time is generally well spent.

UNDERSTANDING AND EXAMINING PERSONAL
BELIEFS ABOUT TEACHING AND SCHOOLING

It is also our belief that many educational issues engage and affect our
heads and our hearts. Teaching is work that entails both thinking and
feeling; those who can reflectively think and feel will find their work
more rewarding and their efforts more successful. Good teachers find
ways to listen to and integrate their passions, beliefs, and judgments. And
so we encourage not only the type of group deliberation just outlined but
also an approach to reading that is attentive to an individual's felt sense or
what some might call "gut" level reactions. In the books in this series that
contain case material and written reactions to that material, along with the
public arguments that pertain to the issues raised, we believe it is essential
that you, the reader, attend to your felt reactions, and attempt to sort out
what those reactions tell you. At times it seems we can predict our reactions to the readings and discussions of this material while at other times it
can invoke reactions and feelings that surprise us. Attending to those issues
in a heartfelt manner, one that is honest and forthright, gives us a better
sense of ourselves as teachers and our understandings of the world. Not only
do students walk into schools with expectations and assumptions formed as
a result of life experiences but so do their teachers. Practicing and prospective teachers can benefit from thinking about their expectations and assumptions. Hopefully, our work will facilitate this sort of reflection.

ABOUT THE BOOKS IN THIS SERIES

The first work in this series, *Reflective* Teaching: An Introduction, intro-
duces the notion of teacher reflection and develops it in relation to the social conditions of schooling. Building on this concept, the second work in

the series, *Culture and Teaching*, encourages a reflection on and examination of issues connected to teaching in a pluralistic society. This work, *Gender and Teaching*, is the third work in the series and examines the central role of gender in teaching and schooling. We were fortunate to enlist Frinde Maher and Janie Ward. They are talented scholars and practitioners and highly respected in the profession. Subsequent works will employ a reflective approach to examine prominent educational issues and to explore further our understanding of teaching. Ofelia Miramontes and Nancy Commins are nearing the completion of their text, *Linguistic Diversity and Teaching*. Other works will include such topics as math instruction and the social conditions of teaching; technology and teaching; democracy and teaching; and emotions and teaching. The structure of the works will vary depending on our various contributors, the content of the work, and the ways we can conceive of encouraging reflective practice. But each of the works will take as its central concern the reflective examination of our educational practice within larger social contexts and conditions.

SERIES ACKNOWLEDGMENTS

Two individuals have been essential to the conception and execution of this series. Kathleen Keller, our first editor at St. Martin's Press (where the series originated), initially suggested that we further develop the ideas outlined in *Teacher Education and the Social Conditions of Schooling* (Liston & Zeichner, 1991). Kathleen was very helpful in the initial stages of this effort and we wish to thank her for that. Naomi Silverman, our current and beloved editor at Lawrence Erlbaum Associates, has patiently and skillfully prodded us along attending to both the "big picture" and the small details. She has been remarkably supportive and capably informative. We are very thankful and indebted to Naomi.

—Daniel P. Liston
—Kenneth M. Zeichner

PREFACE

A book focused on gender and teaching may raise the question in your mind, "What is the issue here?" It may seem to you that because most schools and educational settings are coeducational, girls and boys share most of their courses, and both men and women attend college and graduate schools in almost equal numbers nowadays, sex discrimination is no longer a real area of concern—in the field of education, at least. Or, you may think the gender differences that are left are pretty basic and schools should not and cannot do much about those differences anyway—why should girls want to play football? Other issues, such as multicultural education, or special education, are more pressing. We hope that after you have examined the cases and the issues in this book you will decide that there are important questions worth exploring about gender and teaching and see how gender relates to many other educational topics and concerns. For example, what are the educational expectations about aptitudes, achievement, and behavior that are gender linked, and how do such expectations help or hinder students' actual progress in school? How are male and female students treated by each other? Does it matter whether teachers are male or female? What are and should be the varying roles and responsibilities of students, teachers, administrators, and communities in creating and maintaining these expectations and these relationships?

In short, when is gender "a difference that makes a difference"? In order to visualize an equal education, ought we to ignore and minimize gender differences, or should we emphasize the distinctive qualities of each group and celebrate our diversity? ("Vive la différence!"?) We hope that the cases in this book, and the discussions that follow each case, will help you begin to evolve your own practical theories, explore and perhaps modify some of your basic beliefs and assumptions, and become acquainted with other points of view. This book is *not* about any "contest" between males and females. Although it partly proceeds from our understanding of historical and sociological frameworks that show how women have historically been discriminated against in our schools and in our society, our goal is an education that is equally fair to everyone, boys as well as girls. As Judy Logan, a middle school teacher who writes about her own classes, put it:

> In order to keep teaching about gender from falling into the males versus females trap, I believe it is important to begin by letting students focus on their own attitudes, ideas and feelings. Students need to realize their own habits of stereotyping before they can understand them in the larger society. Like attitudes about race and class, attitudes about gender are sometimes invisible, and we can't analyze them or begin to change them unless we make them visible. (Logan, 1993, p. 21)

We begin, then, by hoping you will explore your own concerns and assumptions about these issues. Then, as noted by the editors of *Culture and Teaching* (Liston & Zeichner, 1996), the second volume in this series, it is important to look outward as well, to proceed on "both an introspective journey and an examination of the social conditions of schooling. We need to know not only what we believe but what schools do" (p. xviii). It is our belief that gender, along with race, class, and culture, is one of the most important dynamics shaping our social structure and the ways all of us make meanings of our lives. Along with race and class, gender divisions also help to create and maintain social and educational inequalities, through institutional arrangements and practices that privilege some people and hurt others. However, there are other views expressed and other conflicts explored in this book as well. We hope that as a result of working with the cases and responses here you will come to understand more about your own attitudes and your own situation in relation to your gender, your race, and your class position as a prospective teacher. We hope you will learn more about the perspectives and attitudes of others in relation to this issue and why they hold the views they do. Finally, we hope that you will want to look further into the connections and intersections of gender with these other structural dynamics and practices—those of race, class, and culture—as you continue your explorations into the social conditions of schooling.

CONTENT AND STRUCTURE

Like *Culture and Teaching*, this book is organized into three basic parts. Part I includes four cases dealing with related aspects of gender and teaching, along with a range of preservice and practicing teachers' and administrators' reactions to each case. Part II is an elaboration of four public arguments pertaining to the issues raised in the cases in Part I. Part III presents our own concluding statement about some of the issues raised throughout the volume, additional exercises for reflection, and a bibliography of additional resources.

The Case Studies

The cases in Part I explore different aspects of gendered experiences in schools. In Case 1, "Sexism and the Classroom," we portray a Hispanic teacher in a small Texas town who is disturbed by her students' sex role stereotyping and has to confront the sexism of the popular culture that now permeates her elementary school classroom. Case 2, "Gender, Race, and Teacher Expectations," concerns the circumstances that contribute to the high numbers of African American boys referred to special education classes. A major problem arises when two teachers disagree about what is best for one young boy. In Case 3, "Who Gets Hurt?", we focus on the teachers' and schools' responsibilities in dealing with recurring instances of sexual harassment and homophobic baiting in a high school class. Finally, in Case 4, "A Woman's Career?", we explore the gendered, racialized, sociocultural aspects of the teaching profession. A young, White, female college senior tries to make sense of the mixed messages from her parents and her teacher training program as she reconsiders her desire to teach.

Each case study is followed by a set of reactions written by prospective and practicing teachers and administrators whom we asked to read and respond to these stories. They represent only some of the many and diverse ways in which people both inside and outside of school systems tend to react to and deal with these issues. Reading their reactions, we can not only see the complexities of these problems and of other people's responses, but we can also perhaps further understand and refine our own positions. In the final section of Part I, we also offer four general reactions to the set of case studies. These general reactions help to connect the particular issues raised by each case to the broader arguments offered in Part II, in which the public arguments are presented.

Between each case study and the reactions, and after the set of reactions for each case study, we have left space in the text for you to write your own reactions and reflections. People approach this task differently. Some find it easier to write their reactions after reading the case study; others find it helpful to wait until they have read others' reactions. We suggest jotting down your reactions in both places. Because the process of learning and reflection is unpredictable and changing, we want to encourage you to make a record of your development over time, as you change your mind, see new perspectives, perhaps change your mind back again, perhaps move in a different direction. We want to encourage you to explore as many different approaches as the case studies, the readers' responses, and your own reactions imply for you.

The Public Arguments

In Part II we move from the particular realm of the case studies to the more general arena of public arguments and present four very different views about gender, teaching, and education. What we call "public arguments" or "public voices" represent clusters of orientations organized around general values rather than sets of hard-and-fast principles to which all who speak in that "voice" must adhere. These summaries represent some basic assumptions that guide their proponents' perspectives on educational policies related to issues of gender. We present *conservative, liberal-progressive, women-centered,* and finally *radical-multicultural* views of culture and teaching. Each of these public arguments has different views about the importance of gender differences and gender discrimination to educational policies and practices. Each also differs in its assessment of the weight that should be placed on gender differences in approaches to educational equity. For example, liberal approaches seek to minimize the basic differences between the sexes, whereas women-centered thinkers tend to emphasize the particular talents and skills of girls and women, which they think have been ignored in schools.

We all live, experience, and continually construct and reconstruct our own and others' gender identities in all aspects of our lives. From our most personal and familial contexts; to our educational and work environments; to our places in the economic, social, and political order—all these are centrally determined by gender. Thus each of the public arguments explored in Part II has implications beyond the classroom and the school, reaching back into our home, family, and personal lives on the one hand and out into the broader political arena on the other. The conservative approach, for example, seeks to maintain or return to a traditional curriculum and pedagogy in the classroom. This curriculum is one in which the Western tradition is valorized in English and social studies and in which topics such as "women's history" or "multicultural issues" are seen as undermining our cohesiveness as a community. Such conservative educational views have their counterpart in a desire to preserve the gender roles of the traditional nuclear family. For each public argument, therefore, we will look at its wider implications, as well as, of course, its specific effects on the experiences of boys and girls, young men and women, and educational practitioners. We hope that our combination of case studies and public arguments will help our readers explore these ramifications on many different levels as they come to locate themselves and others within these debates.

Our Own Views

Finally, in Part III we offer our own readings of the issues associated with gender and teaching and outline a number of ways in which practicing and progressive teachers can continue to explore these topics. We offer a brief introduction to our own perspective, which entails an emphasis on the multicultural, antiracist, antisexist analysis of gender in the schools. Neither of us believes that gender can be addressed outside of the racial, cultural, class, and other contexts that give gender identities and concerns their very diverse sets of meanings. However, neither of us believes that addressing racial and cultural issues is enough without also putting gender at the center of these discussions. Ultimately, we take the position that our schools are places where various forms of inequality flourish and are linked, and we derive much hope from the work of teachers and others in challenging those inequalities and working to build an empowering education for all children. But ours are only two more views, and we encourage you to develop your own. At the end of this section we provide in the Bibliography a list of what we consider to be indispensable books, and we outline some suggestions for further explorations.

ACKNOWLEDGMENTS

Frinde would like to acknowledge the help and support of her partner, John McDermott, her co-author Janie Ward, and all of the feminist scholars and activists whose work has inspired her own in the last 20 years. She would also like to acknowledge the support and patience of Dan Liston and Ken Zeichner, the series editors, and Naomi Silverman, our editor at LEA.

Janie Victoria Ward wishes to thank her friend and co-author Frinde Maher for her support, encouragement, and patience. Thanks also to Dan Liston, Ken Zeichner, and Naomi Silverman, for their editorial wisdom and invaluable guidance. Finally, this book is dedicated to my son Eli who keeps me strong.

I

CASE STUDIES
AND REACTIONS

INTRODUCTION TO CASE 1

The first of our four cases concerns many of the issues facing teachers who wish to create coeducational classroom environments that are equally safe, hospitable, and challenging for both boys and girls. It illustrates the relations between gender socialization, which goes way beyond the classroom, and classroom dynamics, which both reflect and influence gender socialization patterns. Children learn gender role identity and expectations at early ages. Not only do school-age children become aware of gender stereotypes and engage in gendered activities, but they also start to adopt personality characteristics that show the ways they have identified with their understandings of "masculinity" and "femininity." Children use gender differences as a way to organize their social worlds. Because children teach each other to behave according to cultural expectations, same-sex peers also exert a profound influence on how gender is learned. Gender role formation also intersects with race, class, and culture issues, as different attitudes about sex role expectations often have cultural roots and cultural connections.

A related issue is the role of the teacher in combating or reinforcing gendered behaviors in the classroom. What aspects of the teacher's own background and his or her construction of gender come into play? What should teachers do, and why? Although it is safe to assume that all teachers wish to treat their pupils fairly and equitably, the research on curricula and classroom pedagogies, from kindergarten all the way through graduate school, has shown overwhelmingly that girls at every age and from every background do not receive an education equal to that of their male peers. Teachers pay more attention, both positive and negative, to boys. Textbooks, storybooks, and most reading materials feature almost exclusively male activities and heroes. Girls typically get better grades than boys in elementary school, and boys are more likely to be diagnosed as learning disabled and end up in special education settings (see Case 2). However, boys often do better in the higher grades, are more frequently found in advanced-placement classes in high schools, particularly in math and science, and do much better on the Scholastic Aptitude Test.

Furthermore, practices that are central to many school cultures reinforce gender-biased educational experiences. Much is made of gender differences among schoolchildren, from lining up pupils by sex for lunch and recess, to dividing up playground space and activities by gender, to assigning classroom tasks in terms of gender stereotypes. Thus, boys lift and carry heavy boxes, and girls do secretarial errands for the teacher. Finally, girls and boys themselves, through the influences of family, peer, and media cultures, often treat each other with avoidance and hostility. Boys in particular often refuse contact with girls and actively resist assignments and activities they associate with femininity. Studies have shown that when teachers try to call on girls equally, or include more curriculum materials about girls and women, boys will rebel (Sadker & Sadker, 1994; Spender, 1983).

Given these circumstances, teachers who want to enhance gender equity have a difficult set of challenges, including the selection of curriculum materials, the handling of class discussions and the difficulties of intervening in classroom peer group life. This case explores these issues through the specific dilemmas of a second-grade teacher who wants to increase the gender awareness of her class as well as help her pupils get along better with each other.

CASE 1: "SEXISM AND THE CLASSROOM"

Nina Rodriguez steps back from the two large colorful posters of Dolores Huerta, the United Farm Workers Union organizer, and Sally Ride, the nation's first female astronaut, that she has just hung over her desk. She stands for a moment smiling to herself, proud of the way that she has organized and decorated her second-grade classroom. She is especially pleased that the children also seem to like the room. Being late September it is still too early to say for sure, but so far it seems as if this is going to be a very good school year.

Minutes later the second graders come streaming into the room. Recess has ended, and it is time for the boys and girls to take their seats and prepare their desks for reading instruction. Nina asks the children to get into their reading groups.

"Ahhh, Miss Rodriguez, do we have to?"

"Yes, you do."

"But it's not fair!" whines Roberto. "Why do you have to put me and Jose in a group with girls? Why can't we be in an all-boy group, with our friends? I hate girls!"

"Roberto, please," Nina says quickly as she helps the students arrange their desks into small groups of four.

"Yeah, we hate those stupid girls," sneers Jimmy from the corner. "Yeah," echo several more boys, chiming in. "Shut up, you guys," complains 8-year-old Saundra in the middle of a group of girls. "Stupid, yucky boys," whines one of the girls in a taunting, singsong tone.

"Okay, that's enough," cries Nina, with increasing exasperation. "Settle down, now. Open your books and let's get started. Everyone will stay in their assigned groups until I say you can change."

As the children begin to get settled, Nina gives an inward sigh. She knows that she should be used to the back-and-forth baiting and banter of eight-year-olds by now, but she isn't, and this gender-related silliness is especially annoying. Nina had begun her career as a preschool teacher 7 years ago in a Hispanic community on the other side of the state. She worked in a newly established, experimental, and progressive daycare center and preschool that offered teacher education vouchers to the preschool teachers as a way to offset the relatively low wages they received. Nina smartly took advantage of the vouchers and, although it took a long time, combining full-time employment and college courses, she managed to complete an associate's and later a baccalaureate degree in early childhood education. Last year she was hired by the East Newtowne school district as a second-grade teacher, with a class of energetic, primarily recent immigrant youngsters of Hispanic descent.

As a teacher, Nina faced a host of new issues in the move from preschool to elementary education. Along with the obvious differences of age and size, there was little similarity in the ways that the East Newtowne teachers helped guide the children's social and cognitive development, particularly in terms of gender equity. At the preschool there were many opportunities provided for the young children to engage in cross-gender play. The boys played house, and the girls built with blocks, with no problems mixing together in common activities.

Since leaving the preschool, Nina had tried to keep up with the latest research on girls' development. She had been especially interested in the research that found that girls are losing their self-confidence at earlier and earlier ages. In schools, boys become more demanding of teacher attention, while girls become less likely to speak up in class and tend to withdraw. Although she knows that in elementary school girls tend to do better academically, Nina worries about the long-term effects of these early messages on their self-confidence and their academic achievement.

It sure can be difficult to raise competent girls, especially in her cultural community, where traditional gender roles are often quite entrenched. But with the shifts in the economy, it has become increasingly difficult to be a stay-at-home wife and mother. Nina understands these difficulties. When her own father had died, she worked part-time to help the family. She wants more Hispanic girls to be better prepared to become wives, mothers, and paid employees outside of the home. Nina also knows that if girls don't take traditionally "male" courses, such as upper-level math and science, many well-paid careers will be closed to them in the future.

Nina has found that it certainly is hard to counteract the messages about gender roles that the children receive from home, the gendered toys with which they play, and the World Wrestling Federation and Barbie lunch boxes that they bring to school. Even the majority of teachers in East Newtowne Elementary prefer to line the children up by gender, boys on the left, girls on the right. Although Nina is convinced of the importance of gender equity, achieving it in this school with kids at this age feels like swimming upstream.

She turns back to the class. Finally, the children's desks are rearranged, and they settle into their assigned cooperative groups. "Who can tell me what happened at the end of the story that we read yesterday?" Nina begins, to no one in particular. Rose raises her hand and begins to speak. "At the end the hero, ummm, she, I mean he climbs to the top and . . ." Few of the children can hear Rose end her sentence, because a group of the boys starts to giggle out loud. "Miss Rodriguez, Miss Rodriguez, she made a mistake. She said 'she' instead of 'he'!"

"Yeah," laughs Jimmy. "She!! Like a girl can climb the mountain and save the city!"

"Be quiet, Jimmy. You're so immature," calls Marlene as she glances at her friend Rose, looking embarrassed and sitting in silence. "My mom says a girl can do anything a boy can do."

"Miss Rodriguez," calls Bonita over the now-rising laughter of the boys. "Why can't we have a story with a girl hero? Why are all the heros always boys?"

"Why don't we write a story? A story with a girl heroine. We can all work on the storyline together," answers Nina, pleased with herself for thinking so fast on her feet. "Great," call out the girls, but when Nina glances around the room, the boys' faces register shock and disbelief. "Oh, nooooo! No way!" calls Pedro. "Boring," calls Roberto. "Come on, Miss Rodriguez. If the girls are in the story, it wouldn't be exciting at all. They'd be playing house or doing dress up. Girls wouldn't like slay a dragon with a sword."

"Yeah," agrees Juan.

"They wouldn't wanna slay anything," adds Carl.

"My daddy says girls should stay at home and take care of the house," adds Jaime. "This is stupid. We don't wanna write this story, Miss Rodriguez. It wouldn't be any fun. Girls don't do anything interesting."

Nina feels at a complete loss. She hears herself saying, "That's nonsense, Jaime!" and busies herself settling the children down again. For the moment, she thinks, I won't deal with this one, and she turns their attention to the story they are to read next (one, she notes ruefully, with a male protagonist again). But that evening, with a little time to think, she determines to challenge these pupils. Not only do the girls need role models of self-confident, proactive, and successful females, but also the boys need to learn about competent females, maybe even more than the girls do. After all, it is only September, and she hasn't really had a chance to work with these kids very long. She could change the curriculum. She could challenge the classroom dynamics. She could begin to instill in those boys "a little respect!", and she could begin to work on the girls' self-confidence. But how? Sitting after dinner with the usual stack of student journals in front of her, Nina decides she needs some advice, and that evening, knowing she'll never do it if she waits too long, she decides to call a few colleagues.

Dr. Johnson, her best and most caring early-childhood professor, laughs when he hears her voice. "Nina Rodriguez, how nice to hear from you!" Yes, he says, he knows this problem really well, and "it's worse in some communities than others, where the mothers are home and the families are pretty traditional." He goes on, "Why don't you make sure you have some books with girl heroines and then give the students a choice? They don't all have to read the same book—or write the same story, for that matter." He suggests that she then have the students read their stories aloud to each other and make sure that the boys listen when it is the girls' turn. "Boys are always like that, and you just have to be firm with them."

Her next-door neighbor at East Newtowne, a fellow second-grade teacher, is equally sympathetic. "Don't you know it!" Maria Kelly exclaims. "These kids can be really mean to each other, and those boys are so sexist; mine are too. Whatever you do with your storybooks, let me know. We can put up a united front on the playground, maybe, make sure that those bullies leave the girls alone. It's really important to protect the girls, don't you think?" Maria reminds Nina of that workshop they attended a year ago, at which the speaker had recommended a book on caring and education by Nel Noddings as well as *Women's Ways of Knowing*, a book saying that girls learn differently, that they are less competitive, more attuned to relationships with each other than the boys, and like to work with each other in cooperative groups. "You have those learning groups and that's working really well, isn't it? Keep emphasizing that they have to work together. And maybe some days the girls should have their own times together, too."

Yes, Nina thinks, I do want to protect and nurture those girls. Agreeing with both these colleagues, she still feels that something is missing. "I don't just want to protect these girls, I want to empower them. I don't just want to keep the boys away from the girls, I want the boys to learn something, too!" Her final conversation is with her mentor and friend at her old alternative preschool. "How did we get the boys and girls to work together so well?" she asks Dolores Trujillo. "Was it just that they were young?" Dolores laughs and says, "Absolutely not! Remember how we taught them? Remember the rules and how we wrote the curriculum?" And Nina does remember. They had never lined up the children by sex, or made "boy" and "girl" classroom tasks or areas. There had been encouragement of gender-neutral activities, but there had also been explicit lessons about gender awareness. When Nina finishes with Dolores she still feels confused, but not quite so unsure. Maybe she could try some combination of her advisors' ideas. Her past students had been preschoolers; would second graders take to such a direct approach? Is Maria right that they have to take this issue into the playground, too? Should she think about the whole school, or is her classroom the best place to start? What balance of choice, persuasion, and requirements should she choose, so as to avoid alienating the boys too much? And what about the parents? Would they understand and support her? She determines to design her new combination of approaches that very weekend.

READER REACTIONS TO NINA'S SITUATION

REACTIONS TO "SEXISM AND THE CLASSROOM"

Many respondents focused on Nina's actions in the classroom environment. Most expressed the need for teachers to be able to effectively manage sexist attitudes and behaviors. Nearly everyone talked about the need to have explicit conversations with young students about gender roles but noted that these conversations must take place in an atmosphere of trust to avoid backlash. However, as shown later, some respondents also looked beyond Nina's specific actions to ask questions about underlying attitudes as well as about the specific cultural context she and her pupils occupied. Finally, a few also looked outside of her individual classroom and asked questions about the broader community and society.

Nina's Actions

Many people saw the problem as one of inadequate classroom management. This classroom environment has not been conducive to bringing about respect and learning, because the children had not been taught to treat one another in mutually respectful ways. Nina was faulted for failing to address specific sexist remarks, for ignoring disrespect early on, and for her failure to set up and articulate behavioral expectations (with consequences for noncompliance) for the class. As one respondent put it, "She must insist on respect, and call kids on gender-related insults." But suggestions for how to begin ranged from starting "where kids are at," as in single-sex groupings; to helping kids teach one another to be assertive; to a zero-tolerance policy. Respondents also noted the bickering between boys and girls and the devaluing of women and girls. At the heart of it all, they found, were disrespect, lack of trust, and the kids' inability to see the world from the perspective of the other gender. Gender polarities cast males and females as opposites and placed them into two mutually exclusive categories. Some respondents were fearful that children, especially boys, would learn to place a higher value and more prestige on boys and men, seeing one gender as better than the other.

> My first reaction was that of frustration. I have experienced some of the same behavior from the children, and it is hard to change. My students are primarily of Mexican descent. They come from homes with traditional gender roles. I believe that Nina should recognize where the kids are coming from and get them to verbalize it. I would start from discussing similarities and differences and move into acceptance.
>
> —Bilingual Teacher

Nina should have dealt with the issue immediately instead of essentially ignoring it. When she put the students into assigned groups she should have explained the reasons for the groupings. When she said, "That's nonsense, Jaime," she does nothing to address the specifics of what was said; yet when the situation is happening in the classroom that is the most teachable moment. Dr. Johnson makes the sexist suggestion that she has to make sure that the boys listen. (And not vice versa.) Just cracking down on the boys without talking about the deeper issues will instigate more resentment and problems. Maria Kelly's advice to "protect the girls" ignores the deeper issues of students developing respect for one another.

—Former Elementary School Teacher

Nina should follow through on what she says. For example, Nina impulsively suggested that the students write a story together, but because she hadn't really developed her plan, she let the boys talk her out of the idea. This was unfortunate, because now it appears to students as if they can change the teacher's plans by complaining about the assignment.

—Middle School Resource Teacher

Nina should begin to build a community of learners in her classroom. The first step would be to do some team-building activities with the second graders. These activities will build trust and respect among the girls and boys in the class. The class could generate a list of class rules to control the outspokenness. During teaching, strategies to randomly call on students could be employed. The children would quickly learn that callouts are not accepted and that all students are expected to respond.

—Higher Education Administrator

Whereas the foregoing section includes general comments and criticism, many respondents offered specific helpful suggestions about what Nina could do in the classroom to challenge conventional gender stereotypes and promote gender equity. People noted the contributions of teachers in reinforcing gendered behavior. They criticized books with traditional occupational roles and pointed out the ways in which women are underrepresented in textbooks. Specific suggestions included team-building activities, augmenting existing curricular materials with readings and assignments designed to reduce gender bias, and exposure to models of masculine and feminine behaviors and achievements that challenge and disprove stereotypes.

Nina's dilemma is probably quite common because it does seem that many of the old educational materials are boy centered. In my last class, I also found that boys were unhappy when they found out that the main character in one of their required readings was a girl. With children this age I do feel that some outright conversations about gender roles could be helpful. Second graders can also do some really basic research on interesting women, or women from the community could come in to talk with the class about what they do. Any of these activities could be done independently or as part of an already-planned curriculum unit. An essential part of Nina's plan will be the message that she conveys. If she feels that this issue is important, she needs to insist that within her classroom children are respectful of one another. She needs to call them on gender-related insults and make her expectations clear. The message that the children get from her outside of the curriculum will be essential to the success of her plan.

—Master of Arts in Teaching Candidate, Elementary

I would allow the students to form their own reading groups. Boys could read about heroes and the girls could read about heroines. When finished they could report back to the entire class. The second group of assigned readings could be about a character of the opposite sex, with explanations of how the experience of reading about heroes and heroines is different. The third time I'd let students choose a story with either a hero or a heroine.

—Elementary School Teacher

I believe that the classroom teachers should always balance gender in their curriculum materials. The students should study both male and female examples of heroism and success in all areas, including the political, social, artistic, and scientific realms. The class should also be exposed to common stereotypes, as well as examples which disprove these stereotypes. Basically, Nina needs to set up activities and assignments where both the boys and the girls can observe both sexes having the successes and failures which make everyone, regardless of all else, human.

—MAT Candidate, Elementary

The most important issues are

- That gender differences be understood, tolerated, and even celebrated!
- That the gender/culture issues are explained and also placed in the broader context of the out-of-home culture.
- That the reasons for tolerance and acceptance be discovered and then understood by the students.

Nina should

- Confer with parents of boys of varied ethnic backgrounds.
- Let the students write their own stories and read them to the group.
- Be honest with the students about her concerns and why [she has them].
- Have the students imagine themselves to be a member of the opposite sex and write about a situation as that person.

She could also have the students help look for resource materials and project ideas that suggest ways to reduce/eliminate gender bias. She could send home a newsletter or letter to parents explaining some of the ideas she has, things she'd like to do, and ask for parent comments, reactions, suggestions. Related issues include:

- Parent bias. Be open and honest and allow them to air their ideas and concerns. Acknowledge that some people feel that way but that there are compelling reasons to consider changing negative attitudes. Be specific.
- The school administration's bias—same as above.
- The response/reaction of the community at large.

—Experienced Teacher, All Grades

Attitudes

Some respondents dug below Nina's and the children's actions to wrestle with the basic mind-sets toward gender embedded in all of us. Some shared their personal struggles with sexist attitudes. They saw that sexist beliefs are deeply ingrained in our psyches and reinforced in family and institutional arrangements, resulting in many levels on which sexism must be addressed. Learning about gender discrimination can be central to children's process of identity development, because these lessons affect what kids believe and value, their respect and concern for others, and who they become as people.

Because teachers are such important role models, some people asked what kind of self-analysis is important for teachers to become change agents. Teachers must learn to know and affirm their own values, be willing to accept and give challenges, and model openness and an ongoing process of personal transformation.They must be aware of the subtle messages they convey and struggle against inconsistency. Gender issues must be raised and dealt with openly. The transformational function of consciousness raising came up, and one respondent asked us to think about Nina's journey as a feminist. Finally, attitudes toward gender were connected to cultural expectations as well.

Miss R. is right to empower the girls, not protect them. No one will be there to protect them in the future, so they need to stand up for themselves.

—Prospective Teacher

Nina should begin by being very clear with herself and with her students about her own values and her expectations. Open, honest dialogue will begin to create an atmosphere of trust in dealing with emotionally charged issues. I would also advise her to consider how her own changes have come about. She can expose her students to broad perspectives, challenge and stimulate them to think, question, experience, reflect, and share their views and feelings. She can also provide a role model and set standards for acceptable classroom behavior. But she cannot create the changes in the children. Change is a personal process from within. To be in the process and on a journey of greater awareness is the goal.

—Former Eighth Grade Teacher, Doctoral Candidate

It is difficult to not be sexist as a teacher. Even though I feel that my generation is far more aware of gender inconsistencies, we subconsciously act sexist at times. Often the boys are the most obvious and therefore the most responded to by the teacher. I also sympathize with Nina when she tried to create an assignment for the whole class to write stories containing a female protagonist. I cringe with her as all the boys in the class complained that girls can't be heroines.

—MAT Candidate, Elementary

I recently taught a group of students and took special care to check myself on the information they received and to create an environment that was not sexist. But, I contradicted myself outside of the class (unknowingly) with simple actions like lining students up at recess in boy–girl lines, or splitting the group into boy–girl learning groups. This is really basic, but it shows that there are many levels on which this issue must be addressed.

—MAT Candidate, Elementary

One of the mistakes we make as teachers is that (because of the attention to women's rights in the last decade) we think we have a gender-equitable society because there has been so much attention to women's issues in the last decade. In fact there has been somewhat of a backlash the last few years by those who think we've paid too much attention to female issues at the expense of male rights and needs. We need to be aware that gender problems still exist and can be directly connected to cultural expectations as demonstrated by the reactions of some of these young Hispanic children. There may well be distinct cultural gender expectations, for instance, for young Black males, poor White females, upper class White males, etc.

Classrooms need to have explicit lessons on gender awareness. Teachers need to be aware of subtle messages they give kids. Role playing gender-related situations is a particularly memorable and powerful device for young students. Also ongoing discussions and dialogue are best. Class meetings need to focus on situations that arise in the classroom, on the playground, and even at home. And teachers need to be prepared to defend these discussions to parents who may question the use of school time on viewpoints they don't necessarily support.

—Teacher

With respect to this case, I would like to know more about Nina's journey as a feminist. What were her influences early and later in life? What stimulated her thinking and actions (beyond economic realities) to break down gender stereotypes and gender roles? How did her family respond? Friends? Did her ideas alienate her from her culture? What were the consequences with her students? Is she prepared to discuss the consequences for a boy who is empowered to cook a family meal, or a girl who can fix the family car? In this regard, it is important to understand our own journey, beliefs, level of sexist (racist and homophobic) awareness, and sense of who we are in the world as we turn around to teach children to understand themselves and influence their attitudes and behaviors.

—College Instructor

The Cultural Community

Several of our readers paid close attention to the intersection of culture and gender identity development. Each culture teaches its children its own lessons about gender. Gender expectations are taught to children early in their lives and within a variety of social contexts. Thus children bring to school culturally embedded attitudes about how men and women should think, act, and feel. This case raises important questions about gender socialization and the difficulties that can arise when cultural views about appropriate gender roles conflict. How should Nina respond, and why? In addition, this case warrants a look at the process of change that occurs within and between cultural settings, in this case the attitudes of first- and second-generation immigrant populations toward the changing role of Latina women in U.S. society. Gender meanings shift within cultures and within the individuals of those cultures. Nina, like many young Latina women, lives a bicultural existence, and her reflections on her own shifting perspectives about gender roles allow her a unique vantage point. Finally, Nina is a member of the Latino community, a largely diverse ethnic population of many nationalities and cultures. Several respondents cautioned against prejudging, overgeneralizing, and stereotyping all Latino men as macho or all Latina women as submissive and training their children to be the same.

Nina must examine her own belief system. What is holding her back? There are certain core values American schools must teach children so they can become "good citizens" in our democratic society. Teachers are expected to reinforce American values. Americans claim to respect diversity and tolerate cultural differences. However, when subcultures hold beliefs contrary to the broader American culture, it appears that is where we no longer respect the child's home or ethnic background. We step in and show the child a new way of seeing the world. The value of gender equity becomes more important than the respect for a student's culture and belief system.

—Elementary Teacher

Nina also stated that in her cultural community traditional gender roles are quite often entrenched and that she wanted Hispanic girls to be better prepared to become wives, mothers, and paid employees outside the home. She said it is hard to counteract the messages about gender that the children receive from home and the toys they play with. Should one assume that aspects of their own culture will necessarily coincide and generalize over to a different culture, and even if Nina were of Hispanic descent, should it be assumed that the characteristics associated with her experiences are necessarily that of her Hispanic students? Should a teacher set out to counteract messages that children receive from home? While our own beliefs provide a foundation from which to make decisions, it is important to recognize the point at which these beliefs turn into biases and fail to serve their intended purpose.

—Teacher

I agree with Nina's dilemma in that often young girls get overlooked by the education system. But I disagree in that culturally these young women are at a disadvantage due to predisposed cultural gender roles. As a minority community living in the United States many parents see education as the only way of "moving up." Therefore, parents encourage both girls and boys to pursue educational dreams. If anything, women are encouraged to handle many roles: mother, daughter, sister, wife, career woman, etc.

I realize that my response has been a bit of a tangent on the case study, but as a Latina I feel that I must clearly make a case for my community. Too often are Latinas stereotyped as submissive and Latinos stereotyped as machistas. As more and more immigrants arrive they realize that through education their children can pursue the "American dream." I know because my family is one of those.

—MAT Candidate, Elementary

Outside of the Classroom

Most people felt that Nina should be committed to doing whatever she could to bring about gender equity. However, some noted that this issue cannot just be about changing what goes on in the classroom. Several respondents pointed out that bringing about real change means enlisting the help of other teachers, administrators, and the school. How is one to do this, especially if other teachers aren't there yet? Most people who were concerned with these issues highlighted the fact that Nina must move carefully and judiciously, recognizing that not everyone would be ready or willing to change. The schoolwide implications of working for gender equity would entail a great deal of work. Moreover, although gender equity issues have been given more attention over the last 10 years or so, Nina must remember that some people still don't recognize the need for change. Respondents suggested, for example, that Nina move cautiously to get her colleagues to join with her, perhaps by sharing her successful and creative classroom strategies or by making the discussion of gender equity an agenda item in staff meetings. Also useful are professional development activities such as workshops for teachers and guest lecturers. Finally, several people also mentioned the importance of enlisting assistance from parents and others in the larger community.

I think Maria is right by encouraging gender-neutral activities and by educating both genders about the opposite sex. However, it doesn't end in the classroom. The whole school, parents and community, should be aware of this issue.

—Prospective Teacher

Regardless of how innocuous these comments might have seemed, I would not have let them go by without discussion. I would let the boys know where I stood by letting them hear that I think their comments were inappropriate. I would force discussion among my students. I would speak with parents and ask them to support me in a no-tolerance stance. For me it would not be enough to expose them to literature or do consciousness-raising activities alone. There would be need for supplementation, continued dialogue and support from parents and administrators.

—Teacher

I'd put gender equity on the agenda for staff meetings. If there are no concerns, I probably would not pursue the issue further.

—Teacher

What should happen next? One, Nina should implement her plan and document the events. Later this should be reviewed with her peers from afar and possibly the ones she presently works with. Second, Nina should discuss the ideas with the principal and some coworkers. If they seem supportive or interested, she should consider opening up to the whole staff and attempt schoolwide change. The most important issue in this case is the development of the children. Which way will the teacher encourage or discourage their development? The other important issue is instigating change in a traditional school. How much can Nina handle? Taking the initiative to do this type of work on top of all other expectations of the job is a burden. To establish real change takes meetings, documentation, assessment, and advertisement.

—Bilingual Teacher

Nina should begin informal discussions with some of her peers about the messages they are conveying. Nina could share with staff some creative ways to select children or create lines rather than using gender.

—Middle School Resource Teacher

Nina needs to have a conversation on three different levels. First, let the principal know how she plans to handle the situation. Suggest a faculty meeting. Second, she needs to talk with students' parents. Finally, tackle issue head on with her students with activities, workshops. Also, she must realize that professional development is needed.

—Administrator

READER REACTIONS TO
"SEXISM AND THE CLASSROOM"

SUMMARY AND ADDITIONAL QUESTIONS

This case raises central issues for gender and classroom teaching, namely, how girls and boys may be treated equally and fairly throughout all aspects of school and classroom culture. These include verbal participation, arrangement of seating and other classroom climate considerations, curriculum choices, reading and other assignments, the decoration of the classroom, school policies that may affect classroom gender arrangements, and so on. Some specific questions might be:

- What should be the goals of "gender equal" education? How can they be balanced with respect to racial, class, and cultural diversity?
- What are children learning about gender roles at home, at school, and through the media? How may these sources of influence vary and conflict?
- What is the significance of the students' home environments? How should teachers deal with culturally different models for balancing work, family, and gender roles?
- How much and in what ways should teachers intervene in pupil-to-pupil interactions and peer group life, in regard to gender equity?
- How can teachers make sure that girls participate and are encouraged to speak without losing track (or control) of the boys?
- What approaches are available to help teachers use other ways of distinguishing students besides "girls" and "boys"? (Could they line up for recess alphabetically, for example? Could the class be divided into different teams?)
- What are some specific curricular and pedagogical choices that are available to teachers? What approaches and materials are there for teachers who address the issues of gender equity? What is available in regard to nontraditional role models for girls and boys, for example?
- What would need to happen for girls to feel comfortable doing activities and assignments traditionally associated with boys, or for boys to feel comfortable with "girls'" activities?

INTRODUCTION TO CASE 2

No one disputes the fact that all children some of the time, and some children quite frequently, exhibit unruly, disruptive behaviors both in and outside of classrooms. For teachers, making a determination between what is simply a case of "bad behavior" versus a "disability" can be tricky, because such "clinical" decisions are highly subjective and often influenced by complicated, interacting cultural variables created by race, class, and gender expectations. It has been 25 years since the end of the practice of shutting out or institutionally warehousing children whose physical and/or mental disabilities placed them outside of the educational mainstream. Millions of American children with a full range of physical and mental challenges have been able to gain access to educational services appropriate to their needs within the public school system. But the practice of special education is not without controversy. Increasingly, the decisions and choices made by educators are being closely scrutinized in schools, in the courts and, as the soaring costs of special education threaten to deplete the resources of regular education programs, the public policy arena.

CASE 2: "GENDER, RACE, AND TEACHER EXPECTATIONS"

The bell rings, and the class of fourth-grade students hurriedly collect their textbooks, knapsacks, pencils, and pens and head out into the hallway off to their next class. On his way out the door, Charlie, a 9-year-old African American boy, unsuccessfully tries to slam dunk his social studies textbook into the trash can, which tips over with a loud bang. Trash spills all over the floor. "Charlie!" calls Amy Edwards, as she looks up from her desk. But before she can finish her sentence, Charlie quickly retrieves the textbook, halfheartedly picks up the spilled trash, and rushes into the hallway, calling out loudly to his friends up ahead. Sighing, Amy, the student teacher assigned to this class, walks to the doorway. It's only January 20, and she can tell it's going to be a long semester. She knows it would be wise to clean up the mess before Mrs. Johnson, the classroom teacher, returns. As she's picking up the last few pieces of trash, she sees her principal walking toward her door. Glancing down at the mess, he mumbles, "Don't tell me, I can guess. Charlie Robinson again, right?" Not waiting for an answer, the principal continues:

Ms. Edwards, I need a report from you as quickly as possible. It's about Charlie's status in this class. At Mrs. Johnson's request I had him assessed by the special education [SPED] office, but the SPED director doesn't seem to think his misbehavior is that big a deal. Both teachers can't be right about this situation. Now, you know the kid, you've been assigned to that class all year. Here are two reports to review: One is written by Mrs. Johnson, the other by Mrs. Brown in special education. Read what they say and add your own observations and critique. You're smart, fair, and you seem to understand these kids. I respect your judgment. I'll be waiting for your report.

With that, the principal leaves the room.

Amy throws herself into her chair. This is an awkward situation. Ever since she has returned from a 3-year stint in the Peace Corps, teaching in Guatemala, she has wanted to become a teacher here in the United States. She dreamed of working in a school like this one, a small elementary school, recently made diverse by a district-wide desegregation plan and thus an optimal setting for multicultural experimentation. When she began her internship at the school, everyone told her that Mrs. Johnson was one of the best teachers in the school. Her colleagues recalled that after the gifted program that Mrs. Johnson taught in was phased out, and the voluntary desegregation program was implemented throughout the district, Mrs. Johnson was reassigned back into a regular fourth-grade classroom. Totally committed to the school, she has never once complained about the many transitions she has had to endure. Amy has been grateful to be assigned to Mrs. Johnson's class and pleased to be trained by such a skilled elementary school teacher.

Amy starts to think about how she would respond to the principal's request. She begins by first reading the classroom teacher's report. In it, Mrs. Johnson angrily complained about Charlie's attitude and behavior, frequently labeling him disruptive, nonattentive, hyperkinetic, and loud. Compared to the majority of her students, she saw Charlie's behavior as well outside the norm; in fact she was "surprised" that this student hadn't been flagged earlier. In addition, Mrs. Johnson wrote that Charlie's mother, an employed single parent, had been called to the school frequently about her son's difficulties, yet Charlie's behavior never seemed to improve. Mrs. Johnson concluded that because of Charlie, the classroom was simply too difficult to control. She requested that the SPED office provide him with a separate educational environment "specific" to his deficits. She wanted him out of her class for his own good and for the good of the other students.

As Amy thinks about what she has read, her mind wanders back to the beginning of the year, when she was first introduced to Mrs. Brown, the school's SPED director, and the other members of the SPED team. Amy and Mrs. Brown quickly discovered that they both held degrees from the same graduate school, and that was enough to keep the two women chatting together for quite some time. Way back in September Mrs. Brown had warned Amy that there were a few teachers in the school who appeared to have special difficulties with African American students. "I swear," she said to Amy at the time, "with some of these teachers, if there are two Black boys assigned to a class, at least one of them will be labeled by these women. They are so inflexible. They just can't seem to deal with difference."

Amy opens the second folder and begins reading the official assessment report issued by Mrs. Brown. Much of it reads like a foreign language: There are a series of standardized psychometric test scores and psychological evaluations; reading, spelling, and arithmetic tests; instruments to measure language development; and a social development inventory. From what Amy can recall from her graduate school classes, all of Charlie's scores and evaluations seem to be within the normal range.

As Amy reads the words in the final section of the report, it isn't hard to imagine the frustration Mrs. Brown was feeling. She wrote:

> Mrs. Johnson describes Charlie Robinson's classroom behavior as frequently disruptive and out of control, and has determined that the difficulty he seems to have in slowing down and keeping still is indicative of an "emotional disturbance" or "a related learning disability." However, his academic achievement is at grade level, and once we factor in the gender, race, and class bias embedded in the anglocentric clinical tests we use, the scores are at best ambiguous. When I observed Charles's class as part of my evaluation, I did see a few instances of overly exuberant behavior. However, in my opinion it was nothing that couldn't be handled by a strong teacher whom the children respected. Mrs. Johnson fails to realize that the very behaviors Charlie exhibits "inappropriately" in her classroom are considered quite appropriate, and are indeed expected in his home and community culture.
>
> Charles is a 9-year-old African American male who must by definition negotiate at least two very different cultures, home and school. I know his mother cares deeply for Charles and values his education immensely. But his mother is frustrated by what she feels are the low expectations held in this school for Black boys like Charlie. She has a point. Rather than finding ways to help Charlie focus and self-motivate, the school would prefer to spend all

this time and all these resources to determine his deficiences and exclude him from regular education classes. It is my professional opinion that Charles Robinson's current situation can be best dealt with in the regular classroom and that a specialized placement in this case is not necessary.

Amy closes the SPED folder and sighs deeply. This is definitely not an easy decision. She sympathizes with Mrs. Johnson—Charlie could be a handful, and on some days Amy has to admit that she'd feel a lot better if he were assigned to some other class on the other side of the building. And who knows? Maybe a specially designed program tailored to his needs would be the answer. On the other hand, Mrs. Brown has a point, too. Maybe Mrs. Johnson is overreacting, perhaps because she doesn't really understand boys like Charlie and knows little of the social, cultural, and opportunity factors that shape his thinking and influence his behavior. And how would she? She isn't from their neighborhoods, she's probably never even driven through their communities. And Amy doubts that they taught much about these issues of cultural differences in the teacher preparation program that trained Mrs. Johnson. At that time, more than 25 years ago, efforts at school desegregation were in their early stages, and Black, brown, and linguistic minority children were few and far between in this school district. How would she know that disproportionate numbers of Black boys are regularly assigned to SPED classes, where, because of teacher shortages, unqualified personnel provide substandard and inappropriate instruction and services? And how would she know that the current critique of a large number of the psychometric instruments used in assessment state that they are culturally and gender biased, anglocentric, and inattentive to cultural differences?

Amy is truly perplexed. Mrs. Johnson is a very good teacher, hardworking, professional, and always committed to her students. But maybe knowing the unique characteristics and needs of her students of color, and the sociocultural influences on teaching and learning that their presence in her classroom represents, is beyond her comprehension at this time. "No, that can't be all of it!" Amy hears herself groan. "Let's get real! Charlie is not the only problem here. If kids like Charlie make it impossible for teachers to teach, then doesn't Mrs. Johnson also have a responsibility to the other kids in the class?"

Just then the school bell rings. The children come streaming back into the classroom. Pondering her indecisiveness, Amy wonders what she should write in her report to the principal. From out in the hall she can hear Mrs. Johnson's exasperated cry, "Charlie! For the last time, pleeeze stop that now, go into class and take your seat!"

READER REACTIONS TO AMY'S SITUATION

REACTIONS TO "GENDER, RACE,
AND TEACHER EXPECTATIONS"

U.S. schools have long been segregated by race and social class. Ability grouping (including tracking and self-contained SPED classes) segregates children even more within schools (see Oakes, 1985; Wheelock, 1992). Theoretically, SPED offers individualized learning, small classes, and a focused curriculum, but this is seldom the case. Instead, all too often it means a watered-down curriculum, untrained teachers, and questionable pedagogical practices. Moreover, too many SPED classes are overpopulated with children of color, particularly boys. Critics charge that SPED classes are warehousing Black and brown boys whose teachers are unwilling and unprepared to give them what they need to be successful in school classrooms.

Many of our readers focused on what they felt was needed to turn things around in the regular classroom. Some offered ideas for direct classroom or school-based interventions. Others chose to attend to teachers' attitudes and assumptions as shaped by racial bias, which they saw as contributing to the problem at hand. Eitzen and Baca-Zinn (1998) argue that gender works with the inequalities of race, class, and sexuality to produce different experiences for all women and men. Although gender divisions make women unequal to men, different groups of men exhibit varying degrees of power, and different groups of women exhibit varying levels of inequality. As readers discovered and pointed out, this case is not only about African American boys but also about differences in power among various female players.

Intervention

The majority of comments readers made were about Mrs. Johnson's difficulty in handling Charlie. Charlie's behavior, his inability to sit still, and his low impulse control were acknowledged by nearly everyone as particularly challenging. One disruptive child can wreak havoc on an entire classroom. Many saw the problem as Mrs. Johnson's inexperience with these types of students, particularly African American boys like Charlie. Some of the proposed solutions focus on what Mrs. Johnson could do in the classroom. Other readers suggested that to be effective with such students requires culturally specific and relevant knowledge. Knowing the students whom one teaches, their families, their communities, and their cultural environments is essential to being effective with the Charlies of this world. Several suggestions were offered.

The key issue here is who should change? Charlie, or the teacher? On the one hand, the system (teacher) should be working to meet the needs of the child. On the other hand, Charlie has many years of school ahead of him, and his disruptive behavior will not always be tolerated, especially as he gets into middle and high school. Is the school doing Charlie a disservice if they choose to allow his behavior?

Probably what needs to happen is finding some middle ground. Mrs. Johnson clearly needs some professional development on how to handle difficult students. With the help of the school psychologists, Charlie might be able to learn some strategies for working with difficult teachers. It is likely that he will encounter more of them in the future. In addition, Charlie might be able to transfer these skills into other parts of his life, like when he encounters a difficult boss in the workforce.

—School Administrator

The most important issues in this case concern Mrs. Johnson's perceptions of Charlie and other African American students and whether Charlie should be in a special education class or not. Mrs. Brown's report suggests that he should not be. She reports that his test scores reveal that he doesn't need any special education environment to learn, and she suggests Mrs. Johnson isn't really attuned to the experiences and needs of African American boys, which is part of the whole problem (rather than Charlie being the entire "problem"). The question really is, to what extent should Mrs. Johnson be expected to meet Charlie halfway? Does she bear any responsibility in the situation? Can she do anything in the classroom to help the situation get better? The main issue concerns how to challenge the rigidity and narrowness of her perception while keeping in mind that Charlie is indeed disruptive at times and makes teaching very difficult at times. It's a complicated situation. Solving it through special education governmentality isn't the solution.

—Teacher

Mrs. Johnson must not give up on Charlie yet. If Charlie continues to misbehave, Mrs. Johnson could suggest that he take time-outs in the hallway or in a quiet part of the room until he regains control of himself. Another alternative is to have Charlie meet with a counselor once a week to talk about his feelings and discuss his positive or negative behaviors. Or maybe a positive reward system could be implemented so that Charlie can earn points based on predetermined tasks or behaviors that are attainable for Charlie every day. At the end of the week, depending on how many points he earns, Charlie can get some kind of predetermined reward. This way Charlie has something to work toward and to be excited about each week.

Not only might this motivate Charlie to start behaving properly, it will build a relationship between Mrs. Johnson and Charlie. The plan can be created with Charlie, his mom, Amy, and Mrs. Johnson so that everyone is aware of the expectations and so that Charlie is in agreement with them.

—Prospective Teacher

Mrs. Johnson should familiarize herself with Charlie's environment and culture, then document her interaction with Charlie versus a "good student."

—Bilingual Teacher

I'd ask Mrs. Johnson to try treating Charlie and perhaps the whole class like gifted and talented students. She needs to provide her students with choices, build on students' interests, offer them a highly kinesthetic environment, and challenge her students to use high-level reasoning skills.

—Teacher

Classroom Dynamics

Nearly all of the respondents saw this case at least partly as a behavior management problem, one that is made even more difficult in particularly large schools with large class sizes, such as 25–35 children. Students come to class with varied cultural backgrounds and learning styles. It is very hard for meaningful teaching and learning to take place when the group is stalled because of one individual student's behavior, behavior that may be acceptable, appropriate, or easily overlooked in another setting but is terribly distracting in the classroom. Although the first three of the following comments criticize the teacher, several respondents offer more positive suggestions.

The classroom teacher needs help with teaching Charlie in an appropriate manner. He does not belong in a special education class. His classroom teacher needs some new ideas and strategies for assisting Charlie with learning and interacting in the classroom.

—University Administrator

My reaction to this case is one of concern. I feel this is not an effective teacher; she has a definite problem with certain races and she can't see past the color issue here. Charlie should have been moved out of her class and somewhere where he would not always be in trouble. I feel Charlie was acting up because he knew he could push a button. Charlie doesn't have a male role model and he's at a school where the "racial balance" is not what he's used to.

—Teacher

We all have many [kids like this] in our classrooms and skin color is not necessarily an indicator. However, Mrs. J has already made up her mind that Charlie is a failure. Some intervention is needed, with various behavior modifications explored and firm consequences in place for unacceptable behavior. Charlie will never fit into Mrs. Johnson's preconceived mold, but that doesn't mean he can't learn. If he can spend time in another situation for even part of the day, then teacher will retain her sanity.

—Teacher

I've encountered so many so-called "troublemakers" in classrooms where I've taught. Instead of always taking time away from the rest of the students by reprimanding the Charlies, I've tried to enlist Charlie's attention in more active roles in the classroom. For example, I'll ask him to be my helper in even the tiniest way to teach him that he can be active in a positive way. I believe that by empowering a person to believe he or she can excel in a small area we are laying the foundation for achievement in much larger areas in life. Charlie's behavior could have been modified by the amount of attention Mrs. Johnson spent on his good behavior rather than bad. Perhaps all his troublemaking was a cry for attention (even though it was negative). If she were to pay greater attention to his acts of goodness, he'd be learning a valuable lesson in life. So, first of all I'd set the kid up for success, then I'd commend success. I also think that the teacher needs to rethink why Charlie behaves the way he does. Talk to him about ways in which he feels he can be a better student. Come up with a way to discreetly show him when he is behaving improperly.

—Prospective Teacher

Charlie is described as disruptive, nonattentive, hyperkinetic, and loud. These behaviors aren't aggressive or destructive, just out of step with teacher's comfort zone. Perhaps the first question to ask and share honestly together is, What do teachers and students need to learn their best? How can the classroom environment work better for Charlie, the teacher, and all the children? What a wonderful opportunity this class has to learn about differences and community problem solving for peaceful coexistence. Removing Charlie from this class would remove the most vital learning situation that is immediately available.

—Middle School Resource Teacher

Although Charlie is clearly acting inappropriately in the classroom, I do not agree with her decision in alienating Charlie from his class and placing him in a special education class. Perhaps Mrs. Johnson needs to look deeper into Charlie's sociocultural background to see the "factors that shape his thinking and influence his behavior." However, I think that any child, regardless of race or gender, who may be having academic or social difficulties in school can be worked with to achieve success and become more self-motivated. This should be a goal of any teacher, not simply to point out the deficiencies, but to highlight the successes. This is where teachers need to adapt their methods to the needs of the students.

—Prospective Teacher

School Issues

Some respondents looked beyond Charlie's classroom to the whole school environment. One teacher commented, "It appears that Mrs. Johnson and Mrs. Brown don't communicate. The principal should have met with both and tried to collaborate with them over a solution rather than asking Amy to evaluate the situation alone." Most focused on the issues of assessment and teacher professional development, which are closely related because of the difficulties in making distinctions between bad behaviors and genuine learning disabilities. Such judgments are highly subjective and always influenced by interacting cultural variables created by race, class, and gender expectations. Teachers, especially those working with multicultural populations, need to be well prepared.

Assessment

Several respondents zeroed in on the issue of the subjectivity of testing and voiced concerns that standardized tests are ethnocentric, culturally biased, and assume a White, middle-class experience. Preconceived notions of ability could cloud evaluator judgment and produce incorrect diagnoses. As one of our readers wrote, "It was very unfair of the principal to unload such a task onto a beginning teacher." Even Amy herself might hold unexamined biases as her judgment, too, could be clouded by the respect she holds for her mentoring teacher.

The most important issues in the case are the correct diagnosis of students' needs, old-fashioned teaching styles that don't meet the needs of all students, and the dual role students are forced to juggle in their academic career. Of these, I have been personally struggling lately to better understand what particular students must go through on a daily basis and how I can adapt my teaching to their individual needs. One thing that I have learned is the danger of making assumptions about students or anyone in general for that matter. There are no concrete answers, and sometimes the best analysis leads to the realization of inadequacies as an educator and how to work around that. It is a difficult thing to point the finger at yourself rather than the child and determine when that is truly and honestly the problem.

—Prospective Teacher

The important issues raised in this case are bias against gender and race/ethnicity as well as relationships between teachers and parent/teachers. Bias exists, and when teachers are aware of the bias it opens their eyes to a new world. I would hope Amy would become more aware of her colleagues and her own biased views. Perhaps this experience will open her eyes and make her a better teacher. It also represents an opportunity for teachers to use colleague and/or parent relationships to determine ways of helping students have more academic and behavioral success in the classroom.

—Graduate Student

Whose needs are being served? From what I have read it seems like the teacher's needs are being served. She would have everything to gain by losing Charlie. I do not want to assume anything because she is White and Charlie is Black. But I think someone should assess what Mrs. Johnson has done as a teacher to get across to Charlie. Maybe he should be evaluated by someone else. It appears that the person who initially tested him was already biased.

—Prospective Teacher

I think that Amy needs to explore Mrs. Johnson's views . . . for bias. Also, Amy herself needs to determine if she herself has any bias about Charlie and his gender/race. Amy must realize Mrs. J may be coming from bias or preconceived notions about Charlie and his gender and racial background. An examination of her own views as well as Mrs. Johnson's might provide a valuable place for Amy to start. She also must realize that [Mrs. Brown] may also be coming from a bias as she might be trying to overcompensate for the bias against race and gender.

—Prospective Teacher

Amy is in a difficult position. As a student teacher, Amy's voice shouldn't be the one that determines the fate of a child in her classroom. Her judgment could be clouded by the respect she clearly has for her mentoring teacher.

—Prospective Teacher

I believe this case presents the dilemma that faces every Student Success Team (as they are called in my district) across the country. Last school year I served as the SST coordinator in a middle school of 750 sixth-, seventh-, and eighth-grade students. The question I repeatedly heard from teachers was, "What am I going to do with this boy who exhibits low skills, lacks motivation, and is constantly off task and disturbing others?" In my opinion, this case illustrates a challenge that teachers have with boys in general, and specifically with boys of color. There were very few African American students at my school. Most of the boys identified by teachers as needing testing were Hispanic, although there were a fair number of boys of every ethnicity who elicited teachers' cries of exasperation. Teachers, just like Mrs. Johnson, brought boys into the SST process hoping to have them tested and reassigned to special education classes where the boys would receive individualized help in small classes with teachers who were trained to meet their needs. However, very few reassignments were made. The school psychologist almost always came back to the team with one of three reports: 1. there wasn't a substantial discrepancy between IQ and performance on the assessment, 2. the performance on the assessment fell within the normal range, and 3. the student couldn't be tested because the assessment instruments were "anglocentric," but from her observations of the student he was correctly placed in mainstream classes.

—Middle School Resource Teacher

Professional Development

Several respondents addressed the need for professional development with the aim of understanding the implications of racial, ethnic, and cultural diversity for schools and classrooms. Desegregation and racial integration require work, preparation, support, and training. These school-based issues should be addressed as a cohesive unit with teachers and administrators working together: "Teachers like Mrs. J need to be respected, built up and supported." Teachers need the information necessary to understand children of color, including gender and racial biases, becoming conscious of varying expectations and the consequences of low expectations, and learning the perils of stereotyping, especially of Black boys. Teachers need to become familiar with culture-based behaviors and differences in learning styles.

I believe that the biggest issue in this case is that the school didn't spend enough time preparing the teachers for the desegregation plan. Mrs. Johnson was asked to make a big transition from gifted program to fourth-grade classroom. Perhaps this transition should have been accompanied with some school support and training. Mrs. Johnson has not yet acquired the tools and information necessary to understand her new students. Regardless of Charlie's academic intelligence and behavioral problems, Mrs. Johnson is clearly struggling with the dynamic. She obviously needs support from the school. This issue is probably happening in other classrooms too. The school needs to start a program with its teachers on racial diversity and identity.

—Prospective Teacher

The school district that Amy is in has undergone a desegregation program that has only recently made the school diverse. Yet, each of these teachers seems unsure as to where they should turn for advice on these issues. Acknowledging and addressing these issues as a cohesive unit, while allowing for the unique contributions of individual members, would allow for creation of a school that is supportive and effective in meeting needs of admin-[istration], teachers, students, and community.

—Teacher

There's a dire need for teacher professional development in understanding the implications of diversity and in building on that knowledge to learn how to effectively differentiate instruction and curriculum. Professional development would help Mrs. Johnson become conscious of the varying expectations teachers have for their students and the consequences of low expectations. Also, she would become aware of the tendency to stereotype boys, especially boys of single parents. Professional development classes should address the wide variety of learning styles and help teachers understand that the appropriateness of certain behaviors varies between cultures. Perhaps Mrs. Johnson could learn to set realistic goals where students are provided with the opportunity to succeed, which often translates into self-motivation.

—Middle School Resource Teacher

Stereotypes, Assumptions, and the Wider Community

The salient issue of racial bias was mentioned by several readers—specifically, as already noted, the sexualized and gendered aspect of racism against Black boys. Some made proposals to provide cultural instruction and sensitivity training for experienced and successful educators so as to, as one reader put it, "shed the dogma of the elitist society they have been inculcated into." Stigmas, labeling, and negative self-fulfilling prophecies related to teacher expectations—all of these practices lead to segregating students by ability. They thus further reinforce expectations that promote the very negative attitudes and behaviors the teachers are trying to avoid. Finally, some felt the issue was much larger than Charlie and his teachers. One reader said, "Getting Charlie out of the classroom or giving Mrs. Johnson sensitivity training merely puts a band-aid over the larger underlying problem (of anglocentrism, complicity, etc.)." The range of thoughtful comments suggests that, beyond confronting stereotypes, we must look at the role of the home and family, along with understanding more fully the complexities of the culture of schooling.

> The key issue here is who should change? Charlie or the teacher? On the one hand, the system (teacher) should be working to meet the needs of the child. On the other hand, Charlie has many years of school ahead of him, and his disruptive behavior will not always be tolerated, especially as he gets into middle and high school.
>
> —School Administrator

> The response to Charlie comes from frustration and fear and a desire to make differences go away. As a teacher working to create equity in schools and in our culture, we must be very aware of the cultural desire to protect ourselves and create "others" to guard ourselves from.
>
> —Teacher

> Why is there a conflict between White female teachers and Black male students? This conversation must be had because there continues to be a hidden understanding that for Black males to make it through the educational system of the United States they must be to a certain extent, emasculated. Unfortunately, this attitude is also spreading to other males of color as more and more attempt to complete their education.
>
> —Prospective Teacher

> All students bring their needs into the classroom. They all have a history both in and out of the school. And they all deserve an education that is consistent with their own individual needs. Making assumptions and falling into stereotypes takes away from the learning process.
>
> —Prospective Teacher

I'd like to see Amy and Mrs. Johnson contact Charlie's mother and ask to make a home visit. After that they could make other visits to his community, perhaps with him along to describe things. Mrs. J needs to see first-hand what life is like for Charlie outside of school.

—College Instructor

What voice does Charlie's mother have in the matter? Does she know her child is being evaluated to be placed in SPED? Unfortunately, I think that the teachers are failing to use Charlie's mother as she seems to be concerned about her child and could be used as an ally in affecting Charlie's behavior. This case sounds all too familiar in an urban school setting. The majority of teachers in most urban areas are White, while their students are not. The culture clash is inevitable. However, its not just "White culture" that is at issue. The culture of schooling is ingrained in many of us. Even people of color hold beliefs about what school is supposed to be like—[for example,] straight rows, quiet students, etc. These beliefs continue to foster attitudes about how students and teachers should behave under certain circumstances. Many kids like Charlie get caught in the middle.

—School Administrator

READER REACTIONS TO "GENDER, RACE, AND TEACHER EXPECTATIONS"

SUMMARY AND ADDITIONAL QUESTIONS

This case raises a number of issues involved in the referral, assessment, and placement practices concerning the education of students whose attitude and behavior in school are considered negative, nonconforming, and excessively disruptive. Proponents of SPED services argue that the assessment of each individual student referred for services should be conducted by a nonbiased, multidisciplinary team. As you see in this case, individual situations are complicated by the confluence of intersecting factors of race, gender, and socioeconomic status.

Although large numbers of students experience their schooling wholly or partly outside of the mainstream, there is overwhelming evidence that low-income, African American male students are disproportionately placed, and thus overrepresented, in SPED classification categories (Chinn & Harris, 1990, Harry & Anderson, 1990). Frequently these boys are referred by White teachers and others who are culturally different from the students themselves. This case not only raises questions about tensions between SPED and classroom teachers but also asks us to think deeply about the preparation of teachers. What preservice and in-service training models can be instituted to make teachers more sensitive to issues of culture when it comes to the assessment of students' classroom behavior and learning styles? This problem is made worse when the services are inadequate.

Some of the questions that arise from this case include:

- What steps can and should Amy take to determine which teacher's report—Mrs. Brown's, the SPED specialist's, or Mrs. Johnson, the classroom teacher's—to accept?
- What additional information does Amy need to make her decision?
- What strategies can Mrs. Johnson adopt to manage Charlie's behavior?
- What are some of the variables contributing to the disproportionate placement of minorities, particularly African American males, into SPED?
- What roles might the race, gender, and social class of the three teachers play in this case?
- Why do so many teachers and prospective teachers lack instruction in SPED?

- How should teachers respond to the widely held concern that some assessment instruments used to determine special needs are gender and culturally biased?
- What kinds of administrative arrangements need to be in place to facilitate proper placement of students in special education?
- What kinds of administrative arrangements need to be in place to improve communication between teachers in SPED and in regular classrooms?
- How can teacher preparation programs increase sensitivity to and awareness of the intersection of cultural difference and placement in academic programs? How can ongoing, in-service, and continuing education programs do the same for veteran teachers?

INTRODUCTION TO CASE 3

This case study focuses on the issues of sexual harassn and teachers' responsibilities for the way students tr schools. The events depicted in the case study illustrate hc mophobia operate and interact with conventional stereoty ... expectations of girls and boys in educational environments. Sexual harassment and bullying diminish many girls' and some boys' self-esteem and sense of personal safety and impede their academic progress. From an early age in elementary school, many children are also victims of homophobic remarks and behavior. Younger children call each other "sissies" and "tomboys"; high schoolers use the terms "fag" and "dyke." A related issue is the degree to which adults can and should intervene in the dynamics of peer culture, which many teachers assume is "off-limits" and not part of their job.

Although these issues are usually treated separately, this case study addresses the ways in which sexual harassment in general, and homophobia as a specific form, are harmful to students and destructive of school climates, and what teachers can and/or should do about harassing situations. Over 80% of high school girls in a recent survey said they had been victims of verbal sexual harassment, and gay and lesbian youth are reported to be the most frequent victims of hate violence and abuse (Lipkin, 1996; Stein & Sjostrum, 1994). To call girls "sluts" in order to ruin their "reputations," to fondle them without consent, shows young women that they have little power in relation to young men. The harassment of gays leads to isolation, self-hatred, and sometimes even suicide and deprives students who are unsure about their sexual identity of a means to explore and express their confusions. More subtly, to call a girl who wears overalls and no make-up, or who is an accomplished athlete, a "dyke," or to call a quiet, studious boy a "fag," not only deprives gay and lesbian students of their rights to be who they want to be but also deprives everyone of alternative positive models of masculinity and femininity. In "Who Gets Hurt?" we see a teacher wrestling with her growing realization of the pervasiveness of the problem in her classroom, her school, and her community. Does it hurt only one student in one class, or is there more at stake to consider?

CASE 3: "WHO GETS HURT?"

Sarah Turner is in her second year of teaching at Elmtown North High School, which is one of two high schools in a predominantly White, middle- to lower-middle-class community. She teaches English to 10th and th graders. This year her course fits perfectly into the schedule of several members of the football team. Sarah is trying to interest them in Shakespeare and has chosen *Macbeth*, hoping its violent and suspenseful plot will keep their attention. Sarah is pretty pleased with the school year so far, but she worries about this class. A few of the students, usually led by the team's fullback, Bobby Angell, seem to enjoy disrupting the class with distracting comments. Kids whose dress, appearance, or beliefs seem unconventional bear the brunt of Bobby's jokes and mean-spirited jabs. Words like *faggot* and *homo* have been fired at a few boys, especially Frank, a quiet and nervous sophomore who is also enrolled in this class. It bothers her to see the pained and embarrassed looks on Frank's face as he tries to fend off such remarks from Bobby and his friends. Sarah knows that such behavior occurs elsewhere in the school as well; she has heard other teachers mention Frank, and not all of them have been sympathetic to him. A few have implied that he is inviting the teasing by his "wimpy" behavior. In her class, though, neither the other students nor Sarah have really paid much attention to this situation so far. Sarah often makes a mental note to address the issue, but so far she has not interfered, having been mainly concerned with keeping the class in order. She often says to colleagues, though, "Boy, when Bobby and his gang are absent, it's a lot easier in there!"

One November afternoon, Sarah observes, from a distance, Bobby and two other boys approaching Frank in the hallway on their way to class. Checking briefly to see if they are being watched, the boys surround him and knock his copy of *Macbeth* to the ground. The boys begin their taunt: "Hey, sweeetie, read it to me! Wanna play Lady Macbeth?" Bobby's friend Jimmy sneers, "Nah, she's too tough for him."

Just then, from the corner of her eye, Sarah sees another class member, Holly, approach the group from the other direction. Holly is pretty outspoken in class and occasionally tells these guys to shut up when they are making too much noise in the back of the room. Recognizing that Frank is cornered and needs help, she now yells, "Cut that out, you jerks!" Hearing this, the boys' attention suddenly shifts. Sarah sees a heavy arm go up and push Holly up against the corridor wall outside the classroom. Sarah heads angrily toward the group just as the boys make a circle around Holly so that Sarah can no longer see her. She hears them suggest that Holly play Lady Macbeth. "Frank can be Macbeth, you can give him a blow job." "Yeah, that'll wake him up, show him what he's missing." The boys' sneers and giggles end abruptly as they notice Sarah coming their way. After much shoving, they all tumble into the classroom, Holly pale and shaken, Frank with his head down, and the other boys looking defiant and embarrassed. Glancing around, Sarah realizes that the whole class has heard this interaction. Holly stumbles to her seat, but Frank bolts suddenly from the room. An eerie silence blankets the class.

With everyone looking at her, Sarah decides she has to say something. As sternly as she can muster, she tells the boys that she will not stand for that kind of language "in my room or outside my room; if you don't settle down immediately you'll each have to come back for detention." She wonders briefly whether they have football practice that day and figures that they must; either because of that threat or because they are a little chagrined at their own behavior, they settle down fairly quietly. Holly has put her head down on her desk, but the rest of the students seem to have let the moment go, and indeed Sarah is surprised to realize that, like them, she has heard so many remarks like these that she thinks "maybe it isn't such a big deal." She decides for the moment to go on with the class.

But throughout the class Sarah's mind is elsewhere. Frank does not appear again that period, and she is worried. What if he stays out of school? Doesn't she have a responsibility to him? What about his parents? Also, what about Holly? She may not feel comfortable coming back either. During her free period several hours later, Sarah also finds herself returning to her last thought, that "it's not such a big deal because it happens all the time." Could it be that that is what makes it a really big deal? "What if we have all become used to something that is really bad for the kids? Does this kind of thing go on in other classes?" Sarah decides to talk with some of her colleagues, and maybe even go and see the football coach later on in the week.

In conversations over the next several days with many teachers, Sarah finds out that there is a wide range of opinions on this problem, but she also notices that everyone has thought about it. Some teachers have had Frank, or a few other students "like him, you know," whom they suspect are gay and "still in the closet." In a conversation in the teachers' room after school that same day she finds that a few, like herself, actually think the whole school atmosphere has gotten "a little out of hand." Her best friend in the English department, Jean Smith, puts it pretty strongly: "This bunch of football players and their friends think they can run the whole show just because they've won a few games. I'm sick and tired of what they get away with." John Franklin, a history teacher, notes that this kind of behavior encourages other boys to pick on kids like Frank and also to pick on girls, especially shyer and less confident ones. "Some of our kids are really sensitive, and why shouldn't kids be allowed to be a little bit different? Not all guys are aggressive jocks and not all girls want to be cheerleaders, thank God!" As Beth Marks, another longtime English teacher, concludes, "It's not just your classes, Sarah. I think the whole school climate has been getting worse recently. It's like no one respects anyone else anymore, not teachers, not kids, not the community, either."

On the other hand, other teachers to whom Sarah mentions the issue see Frank himself, not Bobby and his friends or the school atmosphere, as the problem. She has a very different conversation from the one in the teachers' room with a couple of colleagues she meets during cafeteria duty the day after the incident. "That kid should be able to take a joke"; "he needs toughening up; that's what high school is all about." Moreover, they tell her the problem is outside their control as classroom teachers. "What are you going to do about how they talk to each other outside the class? That's their turf. I have enough trouble maintaining discipline in my own classroom." Or, "Listen, cafeteria duty is bad enough. If I tried to police their conversations I'd be dead meat."

Thinking back over the week on Friday, Sarah is surprised at the variety and intensity of the responses to the issue. She is also a little surprised to find out that although most of the concerned teachers are women like herself, and most of the others are men, not all the men she talked to were happy about the situation either. On the whole she finds herself torn between a kind of relief that maybe it isn't just her own problem after all and a sinking feeling that now that she has found out about this schoolwide situation she really ought to do something more. One of her faculty colleagues had mentioned that he had heard about a gay and lesbian support group at nearby Elmtown South High School. But it occurs to Sarah that although such a group might help certain gay and lesbian youth, it might not do much about the general atmosphere. She decides that the best way to begin is to talk to the gym teacher, and see what he thinks of the problem. Maybe if the football coach, Mr. Silva, could understand how Frank was feeling, he would make an effort to call off Bobby and his friends. After all, she reasons, he has much more influence over them than she does, and maybe he would have some ideas about what further steps might be taken. But when she asks the coach about the situation, he says, laughing, "Those guys are terrible, aren't they? Just feeling their oats, you know, and gym is the worst. They are just letting off steam! They like this class, not so academic and they get to relax a little. What can I do with them? Hey, they could be a lot worse. When I was their age we gave this runty kid in our class a really hard time!"

Sarah leaves for home on Friday in real distress, wondering what possible options she has now. Over the weekend, pondering the conversations she has had, she decides to begin with a situation she has at least some control over: her own classroom. After *Macbeth* the class is going to do a poetry unit, and now she thinks that this unit could concentrate on "diversity poems"—poetry expressing the voices and perspectives of marginalized groups that will include, but not be limited to, gays. She can begin the unit with a lesson on stereotyping and conclude the lesson by designing with the class a conscious and public policy against harassment of any kind by any student against another. Why, one of the hurtful stereotypes she could elicit might be the one about the "dumb jock" football player! The use of the poetry for "consciousness-raising," coupled with a firm classroom ban on prejudicial comments of all kinds, not only would protect Frank and Holly without singling them out but it would also teach the whole class an important set of lessons. Meanwhile, Sarah determines to talk to Frank separately and mention this support group; it will be up to him whether he thinks it might be helpful.

Although Sarah is excited about these plans, she is still worried about what she found out about the mood of the school. Perhaps, she says to herself, separate incidents like what happened to Frank and Holly can be successfully treated on an individual basis when they come up, but perhaps not. She is glad she is an English teacher and can adapt her own curriculum, but should she also talk to colleagues about some schoolwide programs or events? What about the school's reputation with parents and the community, which, right now, she reflects ruefully, is very happy about the success of the football team? She begins to wonder how what messages this community as a whole is sending to its students and how classroom teachers might begin to deal with these messages.

READER REACTIONS TO SARAH'S SITUATION

REACTIONS TO "WHO GETS HURT?"

Sarah's dilemma illustrates the many levels of individual, classroom, school, and community involvements raised when students who do not "fit in," for whatever reasons, are stigmatized by their peers. Responses ranged from advising Sarah to stick to her curriculum, no matter what, all the way through to a call for a commitment on the part of the whole community to confront and transform the atmosphere of the high school. Complex questions arise here over whose responsibility it is to take on such a charged issue. If a classroom teacher cannot resolve the whole problem in her classroom alone, does that mean there is nothing he or she can meaningfully do? In terms of the students, beyond the harassment, what views of appropriate gender roles do they display? What do students' actions say about the pecking order in this high school and its relation to gender dynamics and the "policing" of gender conformity for all students? Most respondents felt that Sarah had responsibilities both in her own classroom and beyond, and we have somewhat arbitrarily split the responses into classroom, school, and community emphases.

Inside-the-Classroom Issues

Most people thought that Sarah needed to intervene in her own classroom, whatever else she did. Respondents discussed the need to protect Holly as well as Frank; to discipline the members of the football team; and, most of all, to create a classroom atmosphere of respect. As for Sarah's curriculum ideas, respondents disagreed about their potential efficacy. Here are some of the issues and questions that arose.

> The real world is that Sarah's job depends on student test scores, so she must focus on content; hopefully there are counselors who could intervene and even run sensitivity training workshops and perhaps provide a support group for Frank. These issues are society's issues and cannot be swept under the carpet with the chalk dust. This year I had a student, a little boy, who enjoys knitting, crocheting, and embroidery. I worry about what will happen to him in middle school. At least he has had a few years of contentment.
> —Elementary School Teacher

> Sarah needs to take a close look at her own feelings of homophobia and sexual harassment so that she can develop her own system of addressing such events. Why do we give so much power to these big bullies? She seems to

be coming to some awareness of the dangers of such activities and language, but I find it interesting that she could outwardly ignore offensive remarks from one student to another regarding gay people and women. What would she have done if she had heard one student call another "nigger"? Would she respond the same way and take so long to come to a solution?

—Teacher

Perhaps the teacher could talk to the class as a whole to determine what their views on people that are different than themselves and discrimination are. It was interesting as out of the four cases this was the only case that involved male teachers (some in positive and some in negative roles). The case also involved the tension between homosexuality and the idea of the "manly" athlete.

—Master of Arts in Teaching Candidate

Sarah should have done more right when the incident happened, not waiting several days to figure it out. It is obvious that students do not respect each other and do not respect their school from the way the teachers talk. That means Sarah's job is even more important. She needs to get her students to start respecting each other in her class. That is the first step before the problem can be addressed as a whole school.

Sarah needs to address her class first and discuss the problem with the students involved. She needs to call the parents of Bobby, Frank, and Holly to make them aware of the situation and to find out more about their individual situations. What makes Bobby that way, and is he like that at home? What do Frank's parents say about him? Are they concerned about the way he acts? Is Holly okay? After talking with the parents, Sarah would have an easier time getting more personal with each of her students. If incidents like this keep occurring in the class she needs to get more people involved (principal, coach, meeting with parents). Her threats need to become actions, and the insensitivity needs to stop in her classroom.

—Teacher

I believe that letting Holly suffer through this harassment was inconsiderate to say the least. Sarah should have spoken to Holly privately after class and apologized for such an issue occurring on campus. Also, she should have asked Holly if she would like to speak with a school counselor. Holly's parents should have been called and informed about the occurrence. Maybe then, Holly's mother or guardian should have spoken to Holly about what she was feeling and what she should do the next time the boys or anyone else harasses her. I feel that Holly was assaulted. She should not be allowed to harbor feelings of guilt or shame, which sometimes are brought about by our cultural attitudes and perceptions of "girls who might have had it coming."

—Elementary School Teacher

I would have two cautionary thoughts for her as she progresses with her plans. First, she has made an assumption that Frank is gay and plans to mention the support group. A more open, accepting approach would be to invest time in getting to know Frank, providing a safe relationship for honest sharing and demonstrating her acceptance. Frank may not be gay. In this story he has not shared this with anyone. Her attempt at support could easily backfire and further alienate Frank. Secondly, while the behavior of the athletes in her class is aggressive and damaging, she needs to seek to understand their inner conflicts and fears as well. To break down the "otherness" means raising awareness and understanding of all the students. This is a difficult task. For the athletes to become aware of the conditioning provided in competitive sports and learn to shift their perspectives off the field will be a challenge. Some positive, successful athletic role models could help here.

Frank represents a tip of an iceberg in terms of dealing with stereotypes and [dis]respectful language/views in a classroom. Although the case takes place in the secondary level, some of the issues are involved in all levels. Sarah needs to make sure that her classroom is a comfortable and a respectful place for students to learn. If students are not comfortable or are not treated respectfully, then the ability of her students to learn may be diminished or even lost (as seen through students' absences due to their discomfort). I think that Sarah should go ahead with her lessons and look at stereotypes (even jocks), but she needs to make sure her objectives are clear to her students as well as for any parents to see. Perhaps by allowing those students who occupy a more popular stereotype to get a taste of the negative sides of the stereotype, she will be able to enlighten this section of the student body.

—MAT Candidate

I think her attempt at doing a unit on "diversity poems" is a great idea. A lesson on stereotyping is a great way to start, and by the end of the unit she can hopefully get the students to see what negative affects harassment of any kind can have on one another. In my mind, if only a few students become more conscious and more accepting of other people's feelings and beliefs, then Sarah will have done her job and been successful. These are great lessons that no student in Elmtown North High School would waste their time hearing.

—Teacher

If Sarah decides to start a "diversity poem" unit in her classroom, I think the students will see right through this, and once again Frank and Holly will take the brunt of the jokes. Sarah will have to be very skillful in setting up this activity so as not to draw attention to any student in her class who might belong to a group.

—Elementary School Teacher

The key is to engage honestly in the process of exploration of values and breaking down the concepts of difference. For those whose voices have been silenced by this aggression, learning to own their voices, to speak their feelings and thoughts honestly will take much courage and growth of self-esteem. A poetry unit could be the perfect venue, if approached openly. We all ultimately learn and change through acceptance from outside and within.

—Middle School Teacher

I like how, as a teacher, she questions ways to address this situation in the classroom. Her poetry lesson seems a little too rationalistic, and she does not address institutionalized heterosexism and sexism enough, but her ideas and questions are a good start. I also like the recognition that remarks which may not seem like such a big deal may be exactly the things that are getting in the way of some students learning the academic material. What I found most interesting was the blending by both students and teachers (including Sarah) of queer sexuality and deviant gender. What about teaching about the regu-lation of the (male) gender—along with the subordination of the female sex (in the role of Holly) and its concomitance with homophobia? This story can question our own assumptions about sexuality, gender, and queerness.

—Graduate Student

School Issues

Many respondents focused on the necessity for schoolwide reforms, and some mentioned the 1999 killings at Columbine High School in Colorado to underscore the need for attention to the problems of students who are marginalized and scapegoated by their peers. One respondent was specifi-cally concerned about the effects of a gay and lesbian support group, fear-ing that such an organization would further stigmatize its members. An-other linked this case directly to the need for an enforceable schoolwide sexual harassment policy. Several went beyond the need to protect Holly and Frank to a wider concern with an atmosphere valorizing the football team and the hierarchies it represents.

Teachers that Sarah spoke with in the case said they had too much to do just controlling their classes. They used that as an excuse as to why they didn't comment on students' insults. The fact is that they won't have control until students feel safe in their classes, which means they do need to monitor what is said. While one teacher can't affect the entire school atmosphere, she can make her classroom a place that is free of hurtful and derogatory comments. Also, once she is conscious of the situation, she can make others aware, as Sarah did. I would hope that in this situation, several teachers brought their concerns to the administration because they are ultimately responsible for enforcing what is and is not acceptable in their community.

Sarah was wise to discuss the subject with a wide variety of her colleagues. It was interesting that overall it was the women who thought the students' conduct needed to be addressed while more of the men seemed satisfied to just "let boys be boys."

The fact is that we have all very recently seen a graphic portrayal of what can happen when harassment goes unchecked. While the incident at Columbine High School is not the norm, it is true that what kids say to one another is extremely powerful and therefore can be extremely detrimental. As people working in the school community, it is essential that we let it be known and TEACH that mistreating other students physically or verbally is not acceptable. There need to be consequences for that type of conduct. As teachers or administrators we need to acknowledge incidents where students are made to feel unsafe. For a teacher to ignore the fact that students in her class are calling others "faggot" or "homo" during class is wrong. By failing to comment on that type of incident, she is condoning it.

—MAT Candidate

It would be interesting to trace the various groups in school who are typically not accepted by their peers. This is especially true due to the recent events in Littleton, Colorado. How do these students deal with the abuse? For those who are resilient and succeed despite the taunting, what qualities or support do they have?

—School Administrator

Whether or not Frank is gay, other students are. To bring in a gay and lesbian support group without initial dialogue and education that supports such a group, and a safe place in which to talk about these issues, will not be effective at the least; and at the most, could be dangerous.

A staggering number of gay teenagers commit suicide every year because of situations like these—where children feel alone, isolated, and bullied, without an avenue to express themselves.

—College Instructor

Where is the principal? Where is the disciplinary action against members of the football team, regardless of who the victims are, their gender, or perceived sexual preference? The message must be sent from administration, staff, and classroom teachers that these types of harassment cannot and will not be tolerated. Where are the principal and the leadership in this school? The school needs to take a position on physical, verbal, and sexual harassment and deal directly with the offenders. I wonder what policies are in place to protect teachers against the same kinds of harassment, and where the law stands on protecting the civil rights of students.

—College Instructor

The adults at this high school are turning their backs on suspendable, possibly expulsionable, offenses. This is very serious and opens the adults at this school up to lawsuits filed by the parents of students like Frank and Holly. Our handbook reads:

"A *hate crime* is any act to cause physical injury, emotional suffering or property damage through intimidation, harassment, racial/ethnic slurs or bigoted epithets, vandalism, force or the threat of force, motivated all or in part by hostility to the victim's gender, real or perceived race, ethnicity, religion or sexual orientation." Consequences for a hate crime infraction may include suspension or expulsion, and the police must be notified.

"Suspension or expulsion will be considered when *assault, battery,* sexual assault or sexual battery is committed on a student." The police must be notified.

"*Sexual harassment* is a form of personal misconduct that undermines the integrity of academic relationships. No individual, either male or female, should be subjected to unsolicited and unwelcome sexual overtures or conduct, either verbal or physical. Sexual harassment is a major offense which may result in disciplinary action as well as legal action." The police must be notified.

I couldn't help but think of Columbine High School in Colorado when I read this case study. The media [have] reported many times about the lack of behavior expectations for the jocks at the school. It has been implied that the shooting spree occurred because two disenfranchised boys were tired of the abuse they had received at the hands of the elitist jocks. This case points out that the adults at this school have very low behavior expectations for the football players. The staff needs to immediately address issues of law and safety among themselves and with the school's students and parents. Where are the administrators at this school? They are legally responsible for carrying out the behavior guidelines of the district.

The staff at this school also needs to learn about the negative implications of stereotyping. Examples of stereotyping behavior:

- Boys won't be interested in a book unless it is filled with suspense and violence.
- Quiet, nervous boys are homosexuals.
- Boys have to "feel their oats" and "let off steam."

—Middle School Teacher

Community Issues

A few respondents situated the high school in the context of wider community responsibilities and concerns. This community must learn to appreciate and celebrate diversity—including, it is implied, more expansive views of gender roles; otherwise, reforms in individual classrooms and even in the high school itself will come to naught.

What should happen next?

- Talk to the principal, guidance counselors. See if anyone else has ideas or plans in the works. Coordinate with them.
- Ask to have a teacher in-service to discuss how and why the whole school should and could work together on these issues. If the negative behavior is pervasive it needs to be addressed throughout the school, not just in her classroom.
- Teacher attitudes must be heard, addressed, and changed where appropriate.
- The collaborative creation of informative handbooks and in-school resources that are made available to students, parents, and the community.
- The collaborative creation of service learning projects that will involve and engage students, teachers, and community in helping to understand, accept, and celebrate the differences of others.

—Experienced Teacher

Sarah may even take a step further in forming discussion groups with students, parents, and others of the community in order to deal with or at least identify the problem which seems to be great in this case's situation. There are a number of steps at different levels Sarah can take, and it is up to each teacher to do what they see as right instead of sitting idly by and tolerating intolerable behavior.

The harassment which occurred in this case is just one terrible part of the overall important issue presented in this case. The message that the community as a whole gives its students is wrong. The separation must be made between, say, the performance of the football team and the behavior of the football team. Of course it can be appreciated if a team does well, but at the same time they can easily be rightly criticized for intolerable behavior. If a community is unwilling to act or even simply tolerate disrespectful behavior, then that community has a lot to learn about itself. [When] individuals take the initiative even at the classroom level, then the community is brought closer to the solution. However, students not only learn from the actions of their teachers during school, but also from even observation of parents and other adults on the larger scale.

—MAT Candidate

READER REACTIONS TO "WHO GETS HURT?"

SUMMARY AND ADDITIONAL QUESTIONS

This case raises many issues related to the ways in which schools, although officially fair to and safe for all students, actually reinforce and even exaggerate the inequalities of the sexual status quo. Sexism and homophobia take place at the individual, classroom, and school levels, not to mention in the surrounding community. Many of the respondents spoke to the need to address issues of stereotyping at the classroom level through both curriculum changes and rules against students' offensive behavior and remarks. A few pointed out that the dominance of the "jocks" needs to be confronted as well. Others explored the schools' responsibilities, both moral and legal, and what changes in school policy are needed to make all students feel safe. Some mentioned Columbine High School and the need to challenge the schoolwide dominance of the football team. Finally, a few noted the necessity to involve the community beyond the school.

Homophobia in schools and its attendant harassment and bullying weigh heavily on students who might be lesbian or gay. The attitudes of teachers, peers, and the curriculum often combine to enforce a regime of silence and ridicule. It is not surprising that gay teens make up a large percentage of adolescent suicides. Homophobia and sexism also make the task of engaging intellectually all their students very hard for teachers. Teachers, particularly female ones, are themselves vulnerable to sexual harassment. Gay teachers have a particularly hard time; if they stay closeted they too are lonely and isolated and miss the chance to help each other and gay students. Yet coming out in many public schools entails real personal and professional risks.

Furthermore, homophobia makes not only gay and lesbian students, but also all students who are unsure about their sexual identity, feel unsafe, isolated, and lonely at a particularly vulnerable time in their lives. Indeed, homophobia is the basis for much of the "policing" of adolescent gender behavior that forces both male and female students to behave in stereotypical and limiting ways. Thus female students learn to dress and act "feminine" in order to attract boys and to be popular with each other, and males who might develop intellectual curiosity, particularly in "female" subjects, such as English, avoid them or hide their interest. Masculinity comes to be equated only with athleticism and sports. Ultimately, students are denied diverse and alternative ways of becoming masculine and feminine.

- What are the responsibilities of individual teachers, administrators, schools, and the wider community in relation to these issues? How can at-risk students be protected?

- Can and should adults ever interfere with peer cultures? Are there adult-driven school policies that reinforce harmful peer attitudes and behaviors?
- What school policies must be undertaken to challenge harmful aspects of school cultures? How can marginalized students be more fairly treated, and how can dominant students, such as members of the football team, be educated and disciplined? How can such reform policies be implemented?

INTRODUCTION TO CASE 4

This case raises complex questions about motives for entering teaching, the daily choices of classroom life, and the nature of the profession as a particularly woman's job. The need for competent teachers continues to grow, and the range and variety of student needs, skills, and interests have never been greater. Students are much more likely to come from diverse ethnic and racial backgrounds and unconventional home situations, and there are many more pupils with learning difficulties to be accommodated within the regular classroom. Teachers thus need to understand many kinds of pupils as well as master increasing amounts of subject matter material and curriculum choices. Reform movements in many states are increasing the educational requirements for classroom teachers to "raise the intellectual standards" of the profession.

On the other hand, although this factor is ignored in the recent reform statements, the status and pay of teachers continue to rank below those of most professions, and the majority of teachers remain women, usually White women. Males recruited into teaching at these levels often receive extra praise and support for taking on a difficult job. By contrast, young women choosing teaching are still routinely assumed to be settling for a second-class career or fall-back option, reflecting their "natural" nurturing abilities, because the more able may now be lawyers, doctors, or businesswomen. Add the cultural, racial, and class differences from their pupils that many beginners experience as they start their teaching careers, and it's no surprise that many wonder why they are there at all. Although many women of color become teachers, the overwhelming majority of the teaching force is still White. Teachers of color face both similar and different challenges, and their stories provide examples for others to follow. (See the Bibliography for works on teachers of color by Beauboeuf-Lafontant, 1999; Delpit, 1995; Foster, 1997; and Ladson-Billings, 1994).

Teaching promises a host of responsibilities and challenges but without commensurate financial and status rewards. The issue here is not simply, "Why go into teaching?" It is not enough to have a genuine concern for pupils, or to love children, which is where many young recruits begin. The case will look at these and other goals, such as intellectual challenge, concern for the wider community, and the desire to make a difference. Through the soul-searching ruminations of one student teacher, this case raises the question of what kinds of knowledge, attitudes, and goals are appropriate for beginners to consider as they make these important career choices. How do race, culture, social class, and gender influence these decisions?

CASE 4: "A WOMAN'S CAREER?"

Halfway through her student teaching semester, it seems like every morning Helen Schwartz wakes up in a completely different mood. Sometimes she is elated at the thought of the day's lessons and the really good idea she has just had about finally reaching the students in that fourth-period class. But sometimes, after a night spent arguing with her father, she wonders why she is working so hard, why she doesn't follow up on that Women in Science program she did last summer, why she is missing half of her senior year, and above all, why she is "throwing away all that tuition when you could be studying to get into grad school!" On mornings like these she ruefully remembers her student debt, a debt it seems she'll never pay back on a teacher's salary.

She especially agonizes over these conversations with her parents because she knows that even though she's an only child, every penny of tuition has been a financial sacrifice. After all, her father had wanted to be a doctor and had to settle for being a social worker, and her mother, who actually *likes* being an elementary school teacher, has always wanted "something more for Helen since she is so smart!" As her father has pointed out, her interest in "changing the world" could be satisfied through science as well as a teaching career. The Women in Science program, offered through a local women's college, was focused around all the research needed in issues of women's health, such as breast cancer, fertility, and menopause. She could make a contribution in any one of those areas, but instead she has decided to pursue teaching.

Sometimes, as a new teacher, she feels as if she is letting the kids down, too; she must seem alien to so many of them; one more White teacher who "doesn't get it" and can't seem to get her classes under control. The pupils come from such different backgrounds than hers, and they are struggling so hard with her. Some days, she can see on their faces looks of pity, condescension, and impatience as they wait for her to try to establish order and get something done. "It's not like you are doing them any big favors," she mutters bitterly to herself. "They'd be much better off without me around!"

But then, some mornings she is re-energized by her conversations with Jane Dexter, her education professor, the instructor who had turned her on to teaching in the first place. Jane had shown her students that the education system in this country is and always has been an important arena for social and historical conflict and change and that schools are one place where people can still make a real difference. "You don't have to live in the sixties, you know, to work for social justice; you just have to be willing to learn a lot and make a lot of mistakes!" Jane had inspired them all with stories and examples of teachers who had succeeded with poor, working-class, and language minority students. "They aren't 'different'; you are; you must learn about their worlds." Jane had pointed out that someone like Helen could turn children on to examining the conditions in their own lives and even to careers in science and could show them all the links between scientific and social issues. "Environmental issues are really important in these urban neighborhoods."

And the teachers Jane spoke about weren't only those well-known models of the heroic teacher, the likes of Jonathan Kozol, or Edward James Olmos in "Stand and Deliver," or Robin Williams in "Dead Poets Society," all male, whose messianic single-handed charismatic authority seemed distant and unapproachable. Some of the most effective ones were actually women, like that teacher Jessica in New York City's Seward Park High School, who managed to get many of her low-income seniors into college (see Freedman, 1990). On better mornings like these, she thinks she might be able to effect some changes like that in her own future classroom.

Harriet Tubman Middle School is one of three middle schools in a large city, about half an hour away from Dawson College, where Helen is a senior biology major and education minor. Helen grew up not too far away from Tubman, which was built and named in the late 1960s as a magnet school to help the city integrate its Black, Hispanic, and White populations. But her suburb was mostly White and, like most middle-class kids in her own school system, she had taken classes and graduated in an almost exclusively White environment. Dawson is a fairly prestigious coed liberal arts college whose students come from all over the East Coast; Helen and her parents consider it an achievement for her to have gone there. At Tubman, however, Helen has been confronting an entirely new world, one for which neither her special-education class nor her multicultural-education course had really prepared her. The school community is almost entirely working class, and the unemployment level, although not bad for an inner-city community, is much higher than in the surrounding suburbs. The student population of sixth, seventh, and eighth graders is 60% Black, 25% Hispanic, and 15% White. The faculty, however, are almost all White; there are four African American teachers, but the only Hispanic teaches bilingual education, and one of the four African American teachers is the special-education teacher. Each grade is divided into several clusters, each of which has English and social studies with one teacher and math and science with another. So Helen really has two cooperating teachers: She teaches general science to two of Mary Kennedy's eighth grades and helps Mary's colleague, Phyllis Kean, in her social studies classes with the same kids.

One day Helen decides to try to make a concrete connection between the ecology topics she has been teaching and the students' real lives outside of school. ("This will be a good day; I have a real plan for fourth period!") It is 2 days before spring vacation, a good time to try something new. Mary has given her the go-ahead to try a complete unit of her own design after vacation, and she is mulling over several ideas. Yesterday's newspaper had an article about water pollution that traced the course of a glass of water from its origin in a reservoir 60 miles from the city center to its destination in local tap water, where it is full of pollutants from passing through so many old and damaged pipes. Maybe the kids could do something on water pollution in their neighborhood! She would find out what their interest level was and be prepared to explore whatever topics came up. Then she could spend the vacation planning a 2-week unit on the subject.

At first things go pretty much according to plan. In an unusual beginning for this rowdy and mischievous group, whose raucous challenges to Helen's authority are typically led by the girls, the students settle quickly down to work in their small groups to work with the Xerox packets she has prepared. But suddenly Marina, a very bright and lively girl, speaks up. Marina is an important force, as Helen has already recognized; she is interested in science, is something of a ringleader, and can make classmates pay attention if she is into the day's lesson.

Now Marina says loudly, "Listen to this!" She quotes from the article: "'Our city's water absorbs iron, copper, and lead from the pipes, producing yellow water, and elevated lead levels that are dangerous to children.' Hey, my cousin ate too much lead paint! They tried to sue the landlord and they didn't get anywhere! Lousy slumlords. Is it in our water, too?"

Suddenly the room is alive with student comments. Helen tries to intervene and asks them to speak in turn, but to no avail, and she realizes after a few minutes that this is a moment she has been waiting for—the students are all really involved in this lesson! She decides to let them just react for a few more minutes.

"Me, too, we must have the same landlord!"

"My mother went down to City Hall—"

"No one cares about us down there—"

"I don't care about the water, what about the junkyards?"

"Hell, what about the drug pushers?"

"Wait!" (this is Marina) "I want to find out what's in our water! Could we do an experiment? You know, like test some water or samples or something?"

"Naah, let's go down to City Hall together—I know my Ma would come!"

"Stupid, this is science class—what's that got to do with City Hall? I wanna find out what's in the water and the paint!"

There are lots of "Yeah, rights" but an equal number of "Nos" at this remark, and Helen quickly decides to ask the class to think of all the things they need to know, and what they might do, in order to improve their water and maybe look at other kinds of pollution in the community. They make a list on the board, including items like the following.

- Test the water in a few apartments.
- Find out who owns this notorious junkyard near the school and get them to clean it up.
- Clean it up ourselves! (Laughter from the group)
- Take samples of water/soil/paint and test them and write a scientific report.
- Contact the newspaper to do a follow-up story on lead paint as well as lead in the water.

Helen is really excited as she makes the list, but there are a few other comments that she does not write down. Some students, including Marina, insist that "this is science class, not social studies! We should stick to science. I don't want to go visit the neighborhood, I know enough about that dump already!" And Helen also hears a few more disturbing points: "She can't help us anyway, she's never even *been* to the neighborhood"; "Yeah, she's probably scared"; "Well she wouldn't be safe there, right?" (laughter); "I'm not going to get my Ma to stick her neck out. She's scared of the landlord, he's always talking about evicting us"; and "I'm tired of outsiders coming snooping around our house. I ain't letting anyone in to look at my paint!"

It is the beginning of spring vacation now, and Helen has some important decisions to make. It's not that she couldn't change her mind, she tells herself, but it seems as if how she decides to spend this week is going to really make a difference in how she thinks about teaching and even whether she goes through with it after all. Both her cooperating teachers, not to mention Jane, have been really supportive in helping her think about the "water unit." It's just that they don't agree! Phyllis and Jane are both thrilled about the possibilities for Helen to really learn more about the community around the school and in a small way to educate herself about her students' lives and problems. Even though her student teaching will end soon, the unit will give her a chance to explore the wider context, which is vital to understanding her own potential role, not only in the classroom but also in the school and the community. Said Jane:

> You have to show them that you care about them and who they are, and let them teach you. Then your unit could really mean something. It's important to have the chance to meet parents, and you know they never come up to the school. This ecology unit can really go somewhere, the kids can pick an issue and publicize it, they can start in our newspaper. They can really make a difference!

Helen can learn to practice some of her social-activist ideals.

Mary is equally excited, but about the possibilities for teaching science, particularly to the girls. "These kids are bright. Some of them are really interested in science, and you can encourage that! Look at that Marina. I bet we could find a lab she could use for those water experiments." So, thinks Helen, which way should the unit go? Should she emphasize the community part or the science part, or could she do some combination? What kind of research does she herself need to do? All in one week!

And, to top it off, on Saturday her biology professor, Professor Tong, calls.

> We are having a meeting next Tuesday for the students we think have a chance at grad school. You could spend some time during your break looking over your courses, what you've taken, to prepare for the GREs. I remember you said you wanted to think about grad school even though you are student teaching.

When Helen hesitated, Professor Tong had become a little brusque, she thought: "Don't throw away this chance, Helen! You'll get rusty if you postpone the exams, it will be much harder to take them in a few years." During the weekly Sunday telephone call from her parents, she has no idea what to say to them. Her father reminds her,

Isn't it about time for you to be thinking about those grad school exams? Remember how excited you were after that program last summer about going into public health? I really can't see why you couldn't do a lot of good in that field, community service and that kind of thing, if that's what you want. You could really make a contribution, Helen.

Hanging up with a sigh, telling them she will call them soon, Helen thinks that she really is going to have to make some kind of decision about her future. What are Helen's choices in this last spring vacation of her senior year, and what factors in her classroom, her school, her family, and her own dreams should she think about as she ponders the possibilities of a teaching career?

READER REACTIONS TO HELEN'S SITUATION

REACTIONS TO "A WOMAN'S CAREER?"

Readers of this case focused on two main areas of concern: Helen's potential abilities as a teacher of these particular children, and whether she herself should become a teacher. Most respondents saw it as an individual decision only, depending on Helen herself; a few, however, saw her dilemma as reflective of the changing roles of women, the status of teachers in our society, and the broader implications of a White middle-class teacher working with children of a different class and culture. It was interesting to note that this case received the fewest responses of any of our case studies. Perhaps this was because it was the last case, or because fewer teachers could relate to it, or because it is a very difficult topic to discuss. Recruitment of teachers, and the responsibilities of the teaching profession, are once again in the public eye, and there is a range of current ideas about how to recruit qualified and talented aspirants like Helen and how to retain them once they start. Respondents suggested many different ways to approach the issue.

Helen's Talents and Interests

Some respondents focused on Helen herself, emphasizing the point, in different ways, that teaching takes a special kind of commitment, as "we are not in it for the money or the panache." They saw her decision as primarily a personal one.

> Helen and I want to teach because we love the personal contact with kids and we want to make science interesting to our students. We are not in it for the money or the panache that comes from a PhD. Science for some undergraduates is a path to a prestigious career in medicine or research, but to others it is simply a way of looking at the world, or a language that allows one to try to communicate with the natural world. She would only regret it if she didn't try. Helen will be wonderful at bringing the lives of her students into discussion and research in science classes.
>
> —Teacher

> She shouldn't be a teacher unless she is fully committed to it. Teaching out of duty will lead to bitterness. She has to make this decision for herself even if it means drowning out all the other voices so she can decide.
>
> —Prospective Teacher

What should happen next? Helen should write her ecology unit and teach it. This will enable her to make a career decision based on how her unit works out with the students. There may be both successes and failures, but she will have some experience implementing her own ideas about what meaningful teaching and learning really is.

—Administrator

If you feel the pull of a career, you should follow it so you don't live with the regrets and "What ifs." If you realize it's not for you, you just shift gears and change directions.

—Former Elementary School Teacher

Helen could combine science and the community through service learning projects. Related issues:

- This project could last longer and be bigger than one unit.
- She can teach AND go to grad school. It's done all the time.
- She can work on the public health issues with her students and use their findings to provide leverage and clout to make needed social change.

—Experienced Teacher

Teaching: A Woman's Career?

Other readers brought up the issues of gender and teaching very directly. Why "waste" a good university education in order to teach, when women can do other things now? And if Helen were a man, would there be as much pressure on her? Some respondents took up the implications of the answers in the previous section to point out that if she is *not* fully committed, she should wait. Many start and leave after several years, wasting the resources put into their training, because of high demands, low rewards, and negative societal attitudes. A few also noted Helen's potential influence on her female students, although one person was not sure this was a good thing. All the respondents thought her choices here were very difficult ones.

I related to Helen's dilemma very closely since I also went through some of the same pressures by friends and family members when I decided to become a teacher. Being the only daughter of eleven children to graduate from the university at that time and go into teaching seemed like a waste of time and spent resources to them.

—Elementary School Teacher

The gender issue is somewhat hidden by the fact that she is an only child and therefore the attention is on her. If she were a boy, would she be left to make decisions more independently? Would her father suggest the women's anatomy areas for a son going into medicine? Would so many people feel a need to push their opinions so forcefully at her rather than respectfully suggest ideas? I can't help but wonder if she would be treated differently if she were a he.

—Bilingual Teacher

I think Helen can make a difference in the lives of her female students regarding issues of women's health. Female students need female science teachers at some point in time so that they can see how a female can interpret and enjoy subject matter that is so inherently male. Science is not just logic and knowledge, it is also intuition and emotion, which is something important to portray to both male and female students.

—Teacher

If she starts by engaging the kids in water analysis, she can consider where to go with the unit. She can hook Marina, and if Marina becomes excited enough to pursue a career in science, Helen will have accomplished a tiny miracle. And where Marina goes, others may follow.

—Elementary School Teacher

I believe all educators should have some type of alternative career prior to entering the classroom, especially women. I don't think it's fair for women to try to influence young girls into science unless they know what they are talking about.

—Prospective Teacher

It seems that the prudent thing for Helen to do is to return to the Women in Science program. If she finds that a career in science is not what she really wants, she can return to teaching, and will be a much stronger teacher as a result (maturity with age, and increased content knowledge). By staying in teaching, she may always wonder, "what if?" I know we need good teachers, but my experience with interns, like the Teach for America folks, is that they come in, do their 2 years, and then leave to do something else. Yes, they are great to have for 2 years, but I think about all of the resources (human and professional development) that are wasted on teachers who just "dabble" at teaching. Since Helen now has an idea about what teaching entails, she can explore other opportunities and return to teaching if that is what she really wants.

—School Administrator

This is a very realistic case. I have heard many of my students complain about the pressure they feel to choose another career path, yet their hearts are true to teaching. The two fields of public health and teaching are both noble career choices for a socially active, conscious young person. It's a shame they are pitted against each other here. The old adage rears its ugly head: It is better to DO science than to TEACH science.

Teaching is a noble profession, yet it is undervalued by society, low paying, and currently the butt of terrific teacher-bashing. Teaching also has the reputation of not attracting the best and brightest students. Although I don't agree with the father's approach, I can understand his motivations. Clearly he doesn't value teaching, probably doesn't value his wife's position as a teacher (perhaps she was limited in her career choices) and is trying to influence Helen's value system as well. It sounds as if she has the "bug," though; when you reach students through their interests, motivations, and intellect—wow! What a rush. Attracting bright students to the profession and making teaching an equally attractive career choice in a competitive market is a key issue.

—College Instructor

Teaching and Broader Issues

Finally, a few respondents brought up the challenges of teaching at a school where the faculty is almost all White and the students are already aware of the great inequities in their environment. How can White teachers come to understand their own positions of privilege so as to genuinely work against their students' conditions of oppression? Helen's choice entails a struggle with these issues as well.

Another important issue I see is the cynicism that the students show when they are trying to figure out the process for their project. This cynicism is a window into how inner-city children perceive the larger world as uncaring and against them. Even though they are only 12/13 years old, these students have already experienced the inequities in their environment.

—Elementary School Teacher

She really needs to analyze why she wants to be a teacher. Would she be able to act in ways to change the world in areas outside public education too? It is also worth exploring further why the faculty at this school is almost all White. What societal structures make this so? What can be done to alter this situation?

—Teacher

There is one struggle which Helen has probably not yet consciously engaged with but perhaps should. This is the struggle between addressing political goals (which are admirable) and acting like a White savior (i.e., the great White wealthy teacher who comes in to educate and empower and raise up and "save" those poor students of color). I believe it is necessary for teachers to want to teach and help traditionally marginalized students (such as economically disadvantaged students and students of color); however, such efforts can reflect a colonialist and patronizing attitude if teachers do not work against their own privileges and racist/classist ideologies/assumptions. Helen, and those who admire or identify with Helen, need to be sure that they are working against these insidious forms of oppression, lest they end up harming the very ones they are trying to help.

—Graduate Student

READER REACTIONS TO
"A WOMAN'S CAREER?"

SUMMARY AND ADDITIONAL QUESTIONS

Helen's case may be examined in two major ways, which are related, and both have to do with her racial, class, and gender position in the school and in society. First is the gendered nature of the teaching role itself. The fact that most teachers are still women has many implications, including the fact that the femininization of teaching continues to make the profession less prestigious and the related loss of authority and status in the classroom and the community. Many of the respondents wrestled with these issues, particularly Helen's potential contributions as a potential female science teacher. She can now take advantage of other career opportunities, open to her as they were not open to her mother, and this new context makes the choice of teaching as a career even more "suspect" for a bright young woman. Helen's pupils do not automatically listen to her; she has to earn their attention and respect before she can accomplish much, and she has to come to terms with herself as an authority figure as well as a "nurturer." However, as the last respondents pointed out, she also has to decide what she can uniquely offer these students, both socially and intellectually, as a White middle-class newcomer to their community. Questions include:

- How can people decide whether to go into teaching as a career?
- How can teaching be made more desirable to young women and men?
- How can teachers learn about cultures unlike their own, learn to understand the dynamics of their own positions of privilege, and foster genuine growth in their students through respect for their communities?

GENERAL RESPONSES TO THE
FOUR CASE STUDIES

Although most of our respondents concentrated on the specific case studies, a few looked at the cases as a whole. One found that they strongly evoked aspects of his own classroom experiences. Another suggested that what all of them had in common was that the teachers postponed immediate action. She wanted us to keep in mind that interventions in the name of greater equality, whether in terms of gender, sexuality, race, or ethnicity, must begin in classrooms with individual teachers. Another pointed out that teacher preparation must involve unlearning racism and sexism as well as becoming familiar with pupils' communities: This is a long and complex process. Finally, we include a response to Case 2 that we think is relevant to all four cases. This teacher wonders about the connections between what may happen in classrooms devoted to equity and what students may encounter in a "real world" that remains hierarchical and unequal. Although pessimistic, this response reminds us that these are societal issues that do not originate only in schools and cannot be solved in the educational arena alone.

As a prospective teacher with some past experience working with children, teachers and all of the social concerns and issues that surround the educational arena, I read these cases and quickly related them to myself by attaching them to a particular event or experience from my past. I found myself constantly thinking "yes, I know how that feels," and "How DO you deal with that situation?" Each case brought up one or in some cases several issues that I have been struggling with as a teacher. Having just finished a month long stint as a student teacher at a local summer program, some of these issues are very fresh in my mind and are things that I have been actively searching for solutions to or new methods to approach. Having worked most recently with a class of second and third graders made up of minority students, predominantly African American, Case #1 and Case #2 stood out in my head as especially relevant to my own experience.

—MAT Candidate

In general, I thought all four cases were marvelous vehicles for introducing the issues and their associated dilemmas. The ambiguities in each case should generate lively classroom debate. In particular, I noted that the teachers in these cases postponed immediate intervention. While that is probably the norm in real classroom situations, it isn't the best way to handle these situations. Furthermore, while it may not be ideal to jump into controversial classroom subjects if you're not prepared for the resistance they almost always generate, NOT responding immediately does implicitly condone "-ist" behaviors and "-isms." Finally, teachers not only must model sensitivity to student differences but also must be proactive about organizing student, faculty, administration, and parent support—because if they don't do it, no one else will. Between the Civil Rights Act ('64) and Title IX ('72) and today, if we're still fighting these same battles, then leaving these issues to the "authorities" hasn't been effective.

—College Professor

Special education courses and multicultural courses are not providing teachers with the necessary preparation to work with students of color. So what else is needed to help prepare future and current teachers to best unlearn the racism (not to mention sexism, hegemonic philosophy, homophobia, and bigoted characteristics of our society) that continues to eat at our society but also glues us all together? Teachers of color as well as White teachers need other preparatory education before entering the classroom and attempting to learn about the nitty-gritty of the communities that they are working with.

—MAT Candidate, Elementary

In the ideal classroom educational equity would be the foundation of every lesson. Each child's "cultural currency" would be used to form a bridge between the learner and the teacher. All children would be taught with his or her preferred learning styles in mind. This classroom would infuse all learners not just with content knowledge but with positive self-images and cultural pride. The learning environment would value and celebrate all children, and by extension all cultures, races, ethnicities, genders, sexual orientations, different abilities, and social classes.

Unfortunately, this notion of educational equity can exist only in a utopian classroom. We live in a world that is fundamentally unjust; every participant in the learning process is a product of that world. Schools are merely microcosms of society. The problematic relationship between teachers and students of different cultural backgrounds mirrors the strained race relations in our society. Should countless students be tossed aside and relegated to the vast wasteland of special education in public schools? Of course not. Should overworked and underpaid teachers be summarily dismissed because they deem these children "unteachable"? Certainly not. The dichotomy between what is best for the individual student and what best serves the majority of students is a complicated one. Many teachers teach classes with 33 students on their rolls. Each of these 33 students comes to class with varied cultures and learning styles. How can meaningful teaching and learning take place when the group is stalled each time an individual exhibits behavior that may be appropriate in his or her community but is distracting in the classroom?

There is no simple answer to this issue. Is special education the only solution for students that cannot achieve success in the regular, sometimes racist and biased, classroom? Would cultural instruction and sensitivity training for teachers alleviate the problem? Can we "teach" experienced and successful educators to shed the dogma of the elitist society they have been inculcated into? Is it fair to teach all children that they will be valued not despite but because of their cultural difference, when the world simply does not work that way? When we tailor learning to each child's needs, then do we not tacitly imply that the world will always accommodate the child when the opposite is often true? In an era of celebrating diversity it will be interesting to see how these children function as adults in the corporate world that demands uniformity. Are we teaching these children to operate within the culture of power or to simply operate within their own culture?

—High School Teacher

READER REACTIONS TO THE
FOUR CASE STUDIES

II

PUBLIC ARGUMENTS

As the authors of the second book in this series, *Culture and Teaching* (Liston & Zeichner, 1996), pointed out, education in most democracies is a "publically funded, state-supported endeavor. . . . Public schools are public institutions and as such they are the focus of much discussion and analysis"—not only at school board meetings but in the community at large. As we write this, in the year 2000, presidential and other candidates are making education a top priority in their campaigns. Yet teacher education is typically limited to preparing people mainly at the school site and primarily for their classroom activities. Most teachers are not taught to think about the implications of what they do in their classrooms for their schools, their communities, or their country.

As a central issue for our homes, our workplaces, our culture, and our public sphere, gender equity is a perfect example of a set of concerns that extend beyond classrooms and schools. Women have made major inroads into almost every previously male-dominated career and now make up half of our country's workforce. Yet they still earn little more than two-thirds of every male-earned dollar and are responsible for the bulk of housework and child care, even when they work full time. This so-called "double day," the persistence of sexual harassment and domestic violence, and persisting cultural stereotypes of "the feminine" all show us that more than 25 years after the failed passage of the Equal Rights Amendment, women are still "the second sex" in our society, and although these are problems and barriers For White middle-class women, they are worse for working-class women and women of color.

These contradictory patterns may also be seen in schools. In 1972, the same year that Congress narrowly failed to approve the Equal Rights Amendment, Congress passed Title IX, mandating equal treatment of girls and boys in all school programs. Ever since then, girls have been in shop classes and boys in domestic science courses and, perhaps more importantly, women's teams have flourished in many sports. Many observers and participants credit women's sports for producing several generations of young women with increased abilities, ambitions, and self-confidence both on and off the field. On the other hand, as this book has shown, gender (and racial and sexual) stereotyping in the classroom, curricula, and the school community remains an issue with many facets. Although formal equalities have been set up by Title IX, or the Americans With Disabilities Act, or the Bilingual Education Act, the working dynamics of gender and other societal inequalities are harder to change. We hope that the case studies presented in this volume have underlined the complexities in the way some of these issues are played out, pointing the way to possible approaches and solutions as well. Our schools are part and parcel of our society. Because schools both reflect and contribute to the social construction of gender and other cultural norms, so teachers, as individuals and as colleagues, may be influential in addressing these issues.

In Part I we presented case studies to highlight various dilemmas connected with the topic of gender and teaching. In Part II we take the issues raised by our cases and respond to, interpret, and articulate them in four very different fashions. We have purposely tried to compose public arguments that represent existing views, and we have tried to represent a broad spectrum. We have prepared "conservative," "liberal-progressive," "women-centered," and "radical-multicultural" public arguments and have entitled them as follows:

"A Conservative View: Upholding Traditional Values and High Standards";

"A Liberal-Progressive View: Education for Equality and Democracy";

"A Women-Centered View: Celebrating Difference";

"A Radical-Multicultural View: Gender, Culture, and Societal Transformation."

In the conservative orientation we emphasize the maintenance of women's important traditional roles in the family and the community and on classrooms that stress discipline, character building, and academic achievement for all children. In the liberal-progressive orientation we focus on the need for schools to promote gender equality as a central feature of a democratic and student-centered educational philosophy. Examining the women-centered approaches has allowed us to look at the qualities of caring, connectedness, and concern for each other, central values of the private sphere that are often missing from our educational philosophies and our classrooms. Finally, the radical-multicultural view emphasizes gender as a key aspect of multifaceted patterns of societal inequalities and suggests how schools and classrooms can promote practices that lead toward social change and social justice.

These views not only represent public arguments about gender, teaching, and schooling, but they also capture features of our own ways of looking at the issues. We hope that an examination and discussion of these public arguments will enable you to make further sense of all the arguments you have read and help you to understand and better articulate your own views. We doubt that any individual's views will fit neatly into any one of these positions. It is most likely that you will find that you share ideas and opinions with two or even three of the public arguments here. To that end we encourage you to "enter" as fully as you can into each point of view, seeking to understand it on its own terms. Then, step back and look at it again, this time with some distance and skepticism.

After presenting each public argument, we raise additional general and specific questions and issues. We do not elaborate a lengthy list but encourage you, especially in your class discussions and analyses, to explore these positions further. We do, however, link each public argument to the cases in Part I. We hope that connection will enable further discussions of the particular incidents in Part I and the general claims made in Part II.

A "CONSERVATIVE VIEW": UPHOLDING TRADITIONAL VALUES AND HIGH STANDARDS

Introduction

We believe that the public schools in our great society are simply not measuring up to the many challenges they face. Education is and always has been the primary means to individual improvement and social advancement in this country. Yet although there is an overwhelming number of education reform proposals put forward at the local, state, and federal levels, and more money is being pumped into our schools than ever before, too many of our children are slipping behind instead. Rather than being held victim to the multiculturalists' political agenda, or swept up in whatever latest reform fad to come down the pike, educators need to get back to basics. Schools should be about individual academic achievement, not the promotion of a victim mentality, particularly in girls and minority group students. Schools play a critical role in socializing youngsters to our nation's beliefs and way of life. Our schools must turn their focus once again to sharing our common knowledge, morality, and truth.

Throughout our history, and until very recently, teachers have both represented and taught to our children the shared values and individual characteristics that we want to see cultivated in the next generation, namely a sense of honor, personal responsibility, and a strong moral character. But today our schools are being taken over by representatives of a host of anti-White, anti-male, anti-family, and anti-religion fanatics. Chief among these groups are feminists, who for a long time have overstated the problems that they see affecting girls in American schools. Their calls to "take care" of girls, like the calls for multiculturalism, are misplaced, divisive, inaccurate, and highly political. These efforts do little more than create havoc in our schools and derail the education process. They offer nothing in the way of improving individual student achievement and indeed offer rhetorical excuses in the place of the hard work that is needed for all children to succeed.

Family Values

The family is the basic glue of society, providing a primary source of stability for both individuals and society itself. The feminist agenda is centered on an attack on the institution of the family and on commonly held and deeply felt family values. By advocating such radical causes as abortion, cohabitation, homosexual rights, and so-called "alternative lifestyles," feminists, falsely claiming to speak for all women, seem hell-bent on unleashing forces that threaten traditional American family life.

The aim of our educational system should be to produce well-educated women and to support them in whatever career choices they may make, even if they choose to stay home or pursue traditional jobs and careers, such as nursing and teaching. However, in today's politically charged environment too many girls, particularly those who choose to maintain traditional roles, feel tremendous pressure from those who would have them believe that their choices are old-fashioned, self-limiting, and damaging to the cause of women's equality. Feminists are selling young girls a bill of goods. They are told that they can do it all and have it all—wife, mother, professional superwoman—with no attention paid to the untenability of such claims or to the dire consequences to society that these promises evoke. Who will be our nurses and our teachers, and who will stay home with our children? Girls and young women should be allowed, even encouraged, to adopt the values, attitudes, and training that will enhance their essential roles as homemakers, wives, and mothers. These roles are invaluable—they provide a critical service to American families and to American society.

Teachers should be positive role models in this regard, preparing youngsters for the important adult roles they must take on. In short, the traditional division of labor by sex contributes to the social order: Men and women both have extremely important, but different, contributions to make to our society.

Differences, Harms, and Wrongs

Quite simply, conservatives believe that the feminists' overemphasis on gender bias in American schools is wrong. For the last 10 years feminists have complained that girls are being shortchanged in American schools. The American Association of University Women report (1992) and its publicity campaign was carefully designed to frighten families into believing that our schools are a toxic environment for girls. Schools apparently squelch their aspirations and damage their self-esteem; they are ignored, silenced, and betrayed. The feminists who perpetuate such dubious claims seek to eliminate what they call *pervasive bias* in educational practices. They see this bias everywhere: in course selection, curricula, testing, even in funding for athletics. They also believe that, like the girls, teachers too are victims (although they often don't know it) who are "oppressed by patriarchy" and thus have subconsciously internalized the sexism and racism that permeate this culture. Teachers are harming girls, contributing to their underachievement and low aspirations.

Feminist demands for gender equity have turned our schools upside down, and to what end? What they fail to comprehend is that girls are not victims; there is no battle of the sexes other than the one they have manufactured for their own gain. In fact, most girls in our schools and in our society are doing just fine. For example, despite what feminists want us to believe, the simple fact is that many girls are not in our upper level math and science courses because they choose not to be there, not because of so-called biased school practices or discriminatory guidance counseling. Why force choices down their throats in the name of a spurious gender equity? Because there are fewer girls in vocational education programs and boys in home economics, does that mean that there is a grand conspiracy to keep them out? Of course not. These choices represent the ways boys and girls are: their different gender interests and characteristics. These choices are normal and natural, and are, except perhaps to these radical feminists, common sense to us all.

At the heart of this debate is the question of whose values will prevail. Schools should continue to promote the shared common values that have kept our families and the institutions of our society together thus far. Decades of research on biological traits and character development show that social harmony and the cultivation of civility in our youth rests on their learning to respect each other's different contributions to our community. Schools have no business implying that women are "unequal" because they are not men, or teaching girls or any other minority group of students to think of themselves as victims. These ideas are dangerous, demoralizing, and foolish. They have no place in our educational system.

Acclaimed Antidotes

Self-Esteem

The feminists claim that girls in this society feel bad about themselves. Their low self-esteem is, so the argument goes, a function of their social status and their continued devaluation. They are said to suffer from a host of frightening psychological problems, from anorexia, to depression, to self-mutilating behaviors. Our girls, they claim, are in pain, and our society is to blame. Perhaps if these feminists would stop making girls feel like victims, because they ought to become or be treated more like boys, then the low self-esteem some girls evidence would disappear. Self-esteem should come from individual advancement, not from group identification. Teaching children to blame their gender or any other group characteristic for their own failures does little to promote anybody's academic achievement.

Curriculum

Beginning in 1992 with the report "Shortchanging Girls, Shortchanging America," published by the American Association of University Women, girls are said to be disadvantaged in our schools (American Association of

University Women, 1992). They say the curriculum is male centered, that assessments and tests are riddled with gender bias, and that boys are called on while girls are ignored in school classrooms across the nation. On the contrary—largely on the basis of this and other questionable data, today's classrooms and curricula have become far too politicized for their own good. A simple perusal of the average high school English class reading list today tells the sad truth. Gone are the days in which teachers had the freedom to support and include the "great works." The traditional classical canon that has stood us well for generations is slowly being supplanted by a host of "warrior authors": anti-White male haters whose bloated claims of oppression simply confuse our children and obscure the truth.

Girls as Victims

We maintain that when you blame other people for your problems, you can't succeed. Whatever happened to personal responsibility? The feminists would have us all believe in their weird and warped conspiracy theory, that men and boys have it all and that women and girls are powerless and unworthy. Indeed, these people, in their desire to pump up the girls, are ignoring the very real problems that boys are facing in schools these days. Fortunately, as Christina Sommers (2000) persuasively argued recently, the feminist myth is finally unraveling. The evidence is mounting that boys are the real victims in our schools. An increasing number of studies show that girls are the group most favored in school, while boys are the ones who suffer most from biased educational practices. Girls do better in language arts and in the humanities. More girls these days are heading to college than their male counterparts. Male students, on the other hand, are more frequently referred for disciplinary action, are found more often in special-education classes, and have much higher school dropout rates.

Our Plan: Academics and Character for All

As should be clear from what we have argued so far, we think that the main business of schools should be academic achievement, as argued by Chester Finn (1991), Dianne Ravitch (2000), and others. America's students are behind in basic skills in the lower grades, and more and more of our high school and college graduates lack exposure to the great works in literature, history, and philosophy that have made up our country's heritage. Our workers need thorough training in the skills needed to compete in an increasingly internationalized workforce, and our leaders need a firm grounding in the classics of Western civilization. Instead of the steady progress in these directions we ought to be seeing, building on the strengths of the past while looking toward a more prosperous and unified future, our schools have fallen victim to a series of foolish gender and culture wars. The result: a watered-down curriculum in the name of "multiculturalism" and "gender equity" and the substitution of a social agenda and "self-esteem building" for the much-needed inculcation of basic skills.

In their concentration on the demands of so-called oppressed and victimized groups such as women and minorities, the schools have also neglected their other primary function, which is character development and moral training. If our schools and cities are falling apart, and if violence, drugs, promiscuity, and teenage motherhood, not to mention unemployment, are destroying our families and neighborhoods, then the solution is to help all our children develop sound moral character, a sense of personal responsibility, and the qualities associated with successful parenting, gainful employment, and engaged citizenship. Where better than our schools to begin? We must reject the mantle of victimization, which blames others for our own problems and does not allow for personal responsibility. Instead, both girls and boys should be encouraged, by direction and example, to cultivate their own talents and interests as they learn to be concerned about the common good. For girls, if this means becoming a wife, mother, or teacher, so much the better. It is the social reforms advocated by feminists, who want to take women away from their traditional roles, that have been the main force behind the destruction of our nuclear families, and this destruction has been one of the major threats to our stability as a nation. It is time for schools to get back to academic progress and to character development before it is too late.

Comments and Questions

"The Conservative View and You"

General Questions

1. What aspects of this viewpoint were appealing to you?
2. What aspects do you disagree with?
3. Do any aspects seem familiar from your knowledge of schooling, or, on the other hand, unrealistic in terms of today's schools?

Specific Questions

1. How can teachers help children achieve academically without understanding their different learning styles and working with these?

Doesn't keeping a common standard for achievement in *all* subjects, and helping *all* students meet that standard, *mean* treating students differently?

2. What is the best way to handle the gender differences that do come up? For example, how would conservatives want to handle unruly boys, or bullies, or passive girls? Conversely, what should one do about girls who want to do math, or boys who want to read poetry?

3. What are the specific ingredients of the moral and character training recommended? In the pressure of time, how can academics and character training both be accomplished?

In the next few paragraphs we return to the case studies and begin briefly to analyze them according to the perspective we just outlined. Do you think our analysis fits how a conservative would view each case? When you look at the specific case analyses below, do you agree with them or not? After thinking about these analyses, do you still feel the same way about the conservative view?

"Sexism and the Classroom"

A conservative might say that Nina should stick to the curriculum, making sure that the students are fairly treated, of course, but not actively intervening either in peer group culture or through curricular innovations. Some would support traditional understandings of gender role activities and orientations and urge Nina to have "girl" and "boy" responsibilities. They might argue that they were supporting the "family values" that they impute to parents in the community. "Boys will be boys and girls should be girls." In any case, Nina should be primarily concerned with her students' academic progress; whatever else she does, she should make sure that all her students learn the basics—reading and writing—and become prepared for the standardized testing program of the district. It is also important that these primarily Hispanic students learn about our common American culture.

"Gender, Race, and Teacher Expectations"

There are a variety of positions taken in the literature on special education and in teachers' practices of student assessment and behavioral management. A conservative would be most concerned with excellence and with maintaining academic standards in the classroom. Misbehaving students like Charlie should be promptly removed from class, because they create problems not only for themselves but also for the other students. Inappropriately behaved students demand the teacher's attention, which in effect diverts her energy from the other, more well-behaved children in the class. On the other hand, some conservatives are concerned about the high cost of educating groups of children in separate, self-contained, special-education classrooms. Not only Amy, but the whole school should adopt more stringent disciplinary and suspension policies and practices to reduce the bad behavior of the special-needs students now retained in the regular classrooms. As for testing and assessment, conservatives would probably support the use of standardized tests, discounting the validity and importance of claims regarding bias. How can students' progress be fairly monitored and compared without the use of such tests?

"Who Gets Hurt?"

Conservatives would say that Sarah should stick to her individual classroom rather than making it an issue for the whole school. Sarah should enforce a strict and comprehensive rule against all kinds of name-calling in her own classroom, but she should maintain the traditional curriculum and not let the students' misbehavior dictate what she teaches. Sarah also could not and should not interfere with the peer culture of the school beyond her class. Although conservatives would be disgusted with the behavior of the football team, they would mainly expect Sarah to enforce the rules of civility and discipline so that her class could get on with learning the curriculum—in this case, *Macbeth*—to the best of their abilities.

"A Woman's Career?"

A conservative would probably argue that teaching still makes a lot of sense for a woman, as it allows for a combination of work and family life that still ranks family considerations high. As for the water unit, Marina is right: Science class is for science, and politics takes away from learning. Another issue concerns the educational needs and abilities of Helen's students and the opportunity to turn them on to scientific knowledge and skills. How should she be thinking about her students' progress? After all, Helen is a teacher and not a community or social worker, and so the students' intellectual development should be her primary concern. A conservative would have Helen primarily focus on excellent students such as Marina, regardless of their gender, class, and culture, with the idea of encouraging their ambitions to "rise above" and go beyond the limitations of their backgrounds.

A "LIBERAL-PROGRESSIVE VIEW":
EDUCATION FOR EQUALITY AND DEMOCRACY

Introduction

As U.S. citizens, we believe that all Americans should have equal social, political, and educational rights and that our public institutions have a broad responsibility to guarantee those rights to all. Our schools and workplaces should be places where individuals are encouraged and rewarded to do their best, regardless of racial, ethnic, disability, age, or gender differences. Unfortunately, our past has bequeathed us a legacy of discrimination and inequality that our laws, public policies, and educational systems have often reflected and perpetuated. As with other settings, our schools must become places where all students, boys and girls, are helped to do their best, where they are treated foremost as individuals, and where the discriminatory practices of the past have no place.

Schools often fall prey to the political and ideological conflicts of the larger society, and gender issues are no exception. Conservatives want to ignore students' individual needs and concentrate on a "one size fits all" curriculum based on traditional models of the past. On the other hand, many reformers, reflecting the cultural and political battles of the 1960s, want to *emphasize* the ways in which students are different from each other because of the societal and cultural groups these students belong to. Reformers think that girls and boys have special interests and concerns, which cause them to think and learn differently. Of course there are differences among students, but the best way to approach these differences is to begin with students' own needs and interests as individuals first, and then build a curriculum and a school community that attends to and fosters both individual and community growth. This is how we can prepare thoughtful and informed citizens, both men and women, to work toward a wider involvement in our democratic society.

Gender Equality in American Society

The women's movement in American history has been through many important phases, and each phase resulted in significant advances for the position of women in our country. Today, more than ever before, women enjoy the same rights and privileges as men in all areas of society. The contemporary women's movement, which began alongside of and as a result of the civil rights movement of the 1960s, was spurred on by the publication of Betty Friedan's classic, *The Feminine Mystique* in 1963. Friedan argued that women who stay at home with their children suffer from boredom, depression, and a sense that their lives are meaningless: the "problem that has no name." The solution, taken up and advocated by organizations such as NOW, the National Organization for Women, is for women to gain full access to the worlds of work, politics, and community life as equal participants with men. Another major event propelling women into the work world was the 1974 Supreme Court's *Roe* v. *Wade* decision, which legalized women's access to abortions. Coupled with the widespread use of the birth control pill beginning in the 1960s, this has meant that women can now choose when to have their children and how many; the "right to choose" is an important slogan of the women's movement.

Congress and state legislatures responded to this newly awakened constituency. Women were included in the Equal Pay Act of 1963 and the Civil Rights Act of 1964, both of which forbid workplace discrimination on the basis of race and gender. No-fault divorce laws were passed in many states. Many businesses instituted child-care programs and maternity leave. And Title IX, which was passed in 1972, provided for equal treatment for girls and boys in school programs. The result of all of these reforms has been an unprecedented participation of women in the labor force, which is now half women (including both part- and full-time workers). There has been an increasing number of women in male-dominated professions, such as medicine and law, as well as in science and engineering. More and more women are entering the political arena as well.

However, there is still much to be done. The "glass ceiling" still exists in many professions, and only a few women have become CEO's or tenured professors in science and engineering. There are still women's and men's jobs—for example, the overwhelming majority of teachers are still women, although there are encouraging signs of more men showing interest in becoming teachers, nurses, and social workers. Above all, the "double day" persists. All women, even those who work full-time, are charged with the major responsibilities for housework and child care. Also, because women still make on average only two-thirds of a man's salary, it is still more likely that their careers will be more vulnerable to family responsibilities. In a fully gender-equal society, neither women nor men would be hindered by lingering sex role stereotyping from pursuing a life that draws on their individual talents and leads to personal satisfaction and fulfillment. Our society can only benefit from encouraging all its members to fully explore a range of options and choices, away from the traditional limitations of gender.

Schools and Gender Stereotypes

Children learn appropriate gender roles very early, first by the way they are treated in the family. Parents hold female children facing them, encouraging them to relate to the caretaker, whereas they tend to hold boys outward to face the world. Girls are praised for being sweet and accommodating, boys for being adventurous and aggressive, and boys in particular are dissuaded from girlish traits. Unfortunately, in spite of the passage of Title IX, school practices have tended to exacerbate these gender differences rather than challenge them. Thus, teachers emphasize differences in the ways that they treat their students. Elementary school teachers give boys much more attention than they give girls, of both positive and negative kinds. This is partly because boys "act up" more than girls, but they are allowed and encouraged to do so: "Boys will be boys." Sex-typed behavior is rewarded, and "drawing outside the lines" is not: Boys are praised for initiative and imagination, girls for obedience and conformity. Teachers have "girl" lines and "boy" lines for lunch and recess and separate play areas outside. Often the boys' area is much bigger, as the girls are expected to play hopscotch and the boys to play competitive games. Teachers usually discourage cross-gender play, partly for fear that the girls will get hurt. As for the curriculum, literature texts include many more male heroes than females, and social studies materials emphasize male exploits over female lives and experiences. Girls are expected to do better in reading and languages, boys in math and science.

In the upper grades these patterns persist, with girls traditionally avoiding math and science courses that are, incidentally, required preparations for many advanced careers. Conversely, girls often do better in English and foreign languages. The curriculum within these high school courses is often gender-biased as well, with few female authors in English and few female topics in social studies and history classes. Teacher–student interaction patterns still favor the boys, partly because it is the boys who are more disruptive in classrooms and thus claim more teacher attention. In spite of Title IX, many schools and school systems emphasize boys' sports at the girls' expense. The popular boys play football, and the popular girls are cheerleaders for them. Junior high and high school girl students are often victims of sexual harassment, although many schools are now instituting sexual harassment policies. Finally, at all levels of schooling, women are the teachers and men are the administrators. Although there are more male elementary schoolteachers than there used to be, gender bias pervades choices of careers in education. The vast majority of elementary school teachers are women, and high school teachers tend to be split along gender lines by subject, with women more common in English and men in math, science, and social studies. The leadership of most school systems, principals, and superintendents, is still predominantly male.

Schools and Classrooms for Equity and Democracy

Many feminist writers on the subject of educational reform want to institute policies and curriculum innovations that would favor the female students and protect them from the effects of male dominance in the classroom and throughout the school. They emphasize girls' victimization at the hands of boys, the lack of women's perspectives in the curriculum and, above all, the competitive world of the classroom that puts girls at a disadvantage. They want to build a more "nurturing" classroom community. Many conservatives, on the other hand, want to emphasize academic achievement for both girls and boys, at the expense of individual differences. They are concerned with high standards for all students and bemoan reformers who want to make the curriculum more "accessible." They think the classics offer the best education for everyone.

We disagree with both of these positions. Although we also advocate strong sexual harassment policies and high behavioral standards, our philosophy emphasizes equality, not differences, and creating classrooms that are responsive to all students as individuals. We want to remove the barriers that have kept women and other groups back from full participation in their education and from equal opportunities to succeed. Thus, we believe teachers should use a whole range of techniques and pedagogies to draw *all* students into active participation, including small collaborative groups where students with different learning styles can thrive. They should practice inclusive discussion management techniques so that no one group dominates day after day. They should confront gender and other forms of stereotyping through exploring these issues with their students. As Judy Logan (1993), the author of a book on her own teaching called *Teaching Stories*, put it, "In order to keep teaching about gender from falling into the males versus females trap, I believe it is important to begin by letting students focus on their own attitudes, ideas and feelings. Students need to realize their own habits of stereotyping before they can understand them in the larger society." (p. 21)

We want to include women's perspectives in the curriculum, because we believe that all groups should be represented in literature and in history, as they are in life itself. In language arts and literature classes, stories and heroes should reflect a whole range of human and cultural experiences and topics, including an equal measure of female heroines. In history class, if the textbook is biased, teachers should bring in materials on girls and women, famous and otherwise, so that all voices are represented. Elementary school teachers should become well versed in ways of breaking down the distances and differences between boys and girls—in the classroom and on the playground as well. Lines can be formed alphabetically, not by gender. Students can learn in cross-gender groupings and be given assignments that place boys in the playhouse and girls in the block area. Teachers can organize coeducational activities in recess as well.

We strongly advocate programs to bring women and girls up to speed in math and science, so that they may take advantage of the career opportunities open to them that were not there before. We urge the development of women's leadership in school settings, because female administrators can be role models for teachers and for students. Title IX must be stringently enforced, as athletics is a primary setting for the growth in self-esteem needed for women to compete on an equal basis with men in our society.

Ultimately, it is not that we believe that all children are alike but that we believe they are different—that is, they are all individuals and have unique talents and interests that teachers have a responsibility to develop in each one. Gender stereotypes of any kind interfere with the range of activities that can spark any child and make him or her interested in learning. We agree with John Dewey, the father of progressive education in our country, who believed in creating pedagogies and curricula that are responsive to the needs of children at different stages of their development and their interests. (See Dewey's classic book, *The Child and the Curriculum/The School and Society* [1902/1956] for a fuller exposition of these seminal ideas.) When each child brings his or her full self to the learning setting, then all will learn from each other, all will benefit, and the shackles of gender stereotyping will fall away. Classrooms organized in these ways will produce both men and women able to take advantage of the full range of opportunities in our society.

Comments and Questions

"The Liberal-Progressive View and You"

General Questions

1. What aspects of this viewpoint were appealing to you?

2. What aspects do you disagree with?

3. Do any aspects seem familiar from your knowledge of schooling, or, on the other hand, unrealistic in terms of today's schools?

Specific Questions

1. How can teachers work on removing gender and other cultural stereotypes and barriers without focusing on them to some extent? How can we create a more equal society if we don't pay specific attention to the differences that have made us unequal?

2. What is the best way to handle gender differences? Should they be downplayed in favor of thinking about students as individuals, or should they be confronted in order to change them?

3. What about academic standards? For example, doesn't making math and science "more accessible" to some students mean watering it down? Isn't keeping a common standard for achievement in *all* subjects, and helping *all* students meet that standard, the real way to show progress for girls (and others)?

4. How can teachers manage to balance the needs of the individual students with the concerns of the classroom community, the school, and the society?

In the next few paragraphs we return to the case studies and begin briefly to analyze them according to the perspective we just outlined. Do you think our analysis fits how a liberal-progressive would view each case? When you look at the specific case analyses that follow, do you agree with them or not? After thinking about these analyses, do you still feel the same way about the liberal-progressive view?

"Sexism and the Classroom"

The liberal-progressive perspective would support "equal access" to all areas of the curriculum and classroom life. Nina should make sure that she calls on the girls as often as she calls on the boys and that the readings have an equal number of male and female heroes and heroines. She should arrange for a variety of ways of putting the girls and the boys together in learning situations. As for the boys' resistance, she should prevail against it on the basis of fairness and equity and not give in to them but rather insist on inclusion of different perspectives in the stories they read. But the most important goal for Nina is to think of her students as individuals and to encourage each one's educational development. That means a delicate balance between protecting the girls and not squelching the boys too much, so that all the students can learn.

"Gender, Race, and Teacher Expectations"

Liberals would support the idea of trying to manage Charlie's behavior within the class, arguing that labeling and separating children from the regular classroom setting contributes to stigma, shame, social rejection, and diminished self-esteem. However, they would be concerned with the other students, too. When a child has been carefully, fairly, and appropriately assessed as being in need of specialized educational services, those services should be available and well staffed with teachers who have particular expertise in instructing children with learning and behavior problems. Liberal-progressives do not challenge the appropriateness of testing to assess students but believe in the careful examination of standardized tests for gender, race, linguistic, and cultural bias. Amy's concern should always be to balance the needs and potentialities of all her students, seeing each one as an individual with particular learning needs and capacities.

"Who Gets Hurt?"

Sarah should pursue an active classroom policy to protect marginalized students like Holly and Frank. She should work out general class rules of fairness and respect with the students and look at her curriculum to make sure that materials on women, gays, and lesbians, as well as other minority groups, are included. Many teachers have learned to emphasize famous women in English and history courses and look for examples of famous authors, politicians, and scientists who are or were gay and lesbian. Sarah should also look into establishing a support group for gay, lesbian, and bisexual youth in the school, in order to counter their low self-esteem, confusion, and isolation. After all, much of gay and lesbian students' oppression occurs outside of the classroom, and they need a place to be themselves. Sarah should also, with like-minded colleagues, push to establish adequate and enforceable sexual harassment policies. They could promote schoolwide curricular and extracurricular interventions to create a more accepting community that tolerates difference. There could be assemblies and special events to promote diversity.

"A Woman's Career?"

Liberal-progressives might be in favor of Helen's taking advantage of all the new opportunities open to women of her generation. They would want to see more qualified women in formerly male careers, such as science, and would welcome more men in teaching. As for her classroom choices, advocates of this perspective would embrace an inclusive cultural pluralism, wanting Helen to stress all the different sides of the water controversy. Another issue concerns the educational needs and abilities of her students. How should she be thinking about those gifted in science and those not—girls especially, but boys as well—in relation to her hopes for them and her concerns about understanding their families and communities? How should she be thinking about their development as individuals? Helen should encourage Marina and the other talented students in their scientific skills, to help them get into the college track in high school. But her major concern should be for the majority of her students and their intellectual progress in relation to science. She should do all she can for the girls previously denied access to science and math skill development.

A "WOMEN-CENTERED VIEW": CELEBRATING DIFFERENCE

Introduction

We believe that our society and our schools must begin to recognize the importance of gender differences and give more attention to women's perspectives on the world. In our society, as in almost all others, women and men have always inhabited different spheres of activity and different frames of reference. In the preindustrial era, when most people worked at home, both men and women had important economic roles and family responsibilities, even though men have always been family heads and controlled the public institutions of church and state. Ever since the Industrial Revolution, however, the division between the sexes, up until recently, has widened. Women have been solely responsible for the private sphere of home, family, and relationships, and men have been responsible for the public sphere of work, politics, and public affairs. Moreover, women's inferior place in society and our long association with mothering and child rearing has rendered us universally vulnerable to male dominance in all aspects of our lives: from economic and political hegemony to domestic violence to the manipulative controls over our bodies in the form of restricted access to birth control, media exploitation, and pornography.

Going along with these societal divisions and exploitations have been sharp differences in men's and women's psychological development, philosophical and moral orientation, and basic attitudes toward life. For example, men have derived their identities from achievements in the public sphere, and women from their relationships with others. Yet because men have dominated the worlds of work, education, and intellectual life for so long, it has been their viewpoints and their knowledge that have shaped the ways we have come to view the world. For example, mothering is demeaned as a "natural activity" that anyone can do, and competition is more valued than connections with others.

These dynamics have profoundly shaped our educational system in myriad ways. Schools have always been places where children are socialized into the knowledge, skills, and attitudes that they will need to succeed in our society—a society where male traits and activities predominate. Thus schools emphasize competition and individual achievement in the ways that educational practices are organized and students rewarded. The curriculum is similarly male centered: Topics in literature and social studies emphasize male exploits in the public sphere. Teachers, who are primarily women because their particular qualities of nurturance well fit them to work with children, are prevented from responding to the interests of all their students, particularly girls, by this overwhelmingly male bias. Female students are also victims of sexual harassment and male bullying in classrooms and playgrounds. We believe that curricula, pedagogies, and school atmospheres all have to change, not only to give voice and support to female students silenced in educational settings but also, more importantly, to educate all children in the values of caring, connection, and community. These values are missing not only from schools but also from all our public institutions, to their great harm. If we start in our schools, we can use the qualities and values associated with women to build a more humane society.

Uncovering the Experiences and Worldviews of Women

Although many feminists trace the origins of their movement back to *The Feminine Mystique* (Friedan, 1963), others begin their stories with the experiences of women as activists in the civil rights and anti-Vietnam War movements. While men wrote the policy statements, confronted the media, and led demonstrations, women were in charge of offices, mimeograph machines, and coffee; even when they were the ones who had gone door to door, listening to constituents and identifying issues, men received the credit. Helped by the groundbreaking works such as Simone De Beauvoir's (1953) classic treatise *The Second Sex*, women in the early and mid-1970s began to argue that the oppression of women was older, deeper, and perhaps more fundamental than race and class oppression, as it was based on biological connections to childbearing and rearing. While women were homebound for specific periods of time, men could hunt, amass property, and make war, as well as making sure that they controlled women as the mothers of their offspring. Human societies were patriarchies, organized around male control of economic resources and political power.

Delving into the implications of these insights about the continuing oppression of women in our society, feminists began to look at a range of issues. Besides working for equal access to education and jobs, they wrote about rape, domestic violence, and pornography, and they worked for laws against marital rape, built battered women's shelters, and began antipornography political campaigns. They also began to challenge the centuries of male domination of the academic disciplines and the education system. As feminist scholars looked at the works of women in literature and the lives of women in history, a growing number began to move away from the previous narrow focus simply on women's oppression. They began to see that one of its chief aspects was the ignoring and demeaning of the activities, experiences, qualities, and values associated with women. Why, for example, are paintings, and not quilting or needlework, considered great art? Why has the literary canon emphasized the epic and the "great novel" over the personal essay and the lyric poem? Why does history record the exploits of great men in the public sphere and not the daily lives of women and men who make up the texture of our past and present lives?

Taking these questions up in the fields of psychology and moral development, scholars such as Nancy Chodorow (1999) and Carol Gilligan (1982) have argued that women and men have a different, and distinctive, orientation to the world. Whereas men develop a morality of justice through their the public sphere activities, women, oriented more to relationships, are more likely to make moral decisions based on care for others. Whereas men focus on rights, women are more concerned with responsibilities. It is not that one of these orientations is better, but that they are different; both are needed for society to work. It has been men's control over the ways we think about the world that has rendered these "women's ways" unnoticed and inferior. It is time, these theorists argue, for a society that pays attention to the values of caring and responsibility. We need to build community and relationships rather than simply promoting competition, achievement, and rampant individualism.

Schools and "Women's Ways of Knowing"

The connections between these ideas and the problems of our schools are obvious. Whether we look at curricula, or children's learning styles, or the value systems in classrooms and schools, the patterns of male dominance hold sway. Schools, like our larger society, are places where too often competition is the primary motivator for learning and where achievement is rewarded according to very limited and limiting standards. Instead of being able to respond to children as individuals, teachers are often forced to impose a standardized curriculum on everyone. Because the hard work of teaching is demeaned by being thought "natural" to women and not requiring much imagination and skill, predominantly male administrators and curriculum specialists take the power out of teachers' hands and dictate what and how they will teach. In elementary schools, where obedience and conformity are often stressed along with competition, girls often do better academically because they tend to be more docile. Teachers pay more attention, both positively and negatively, to boys because they tend to be more active. Nevertheless, elementary school classroom environments have been criticized as being "too feminine," as if boys are oppressed by their female teachers. Actually, it is the personal relationships teachers build with students that help mitigate the harsh demands of a standardized curriculum.

In the higher grades, when sex role stereotypes become much stronger, girls are at an increasing disadvantage academically. Carol Gilligan has shown that, beginning with puberty, girls "fall silent" as they try to meet the contradictory expectations of pleasing others, accommodating male standards for female attractiveness and docility, and yet succeeding academically. Not only do the curricula favor and emphasize the perspectives and achievements of males, but also traditional teaching methods encourage male participation with their emphasis on Socratic questioning and the search for the single "right" answer. Pedagogies built on competitive hand waving silence the quieter students, particularly girls. Mary Belenky, Blythe Clinchy, Nancy Goldberger, and Jill Tarule, in their book *Women's Ways of*

Knowing (1986), suggested that women and girls may learn and think differently from men. Whereas males may prefer to engage in argument and detached analysis, women are more likely to want to make personal connections to a topic and seek to understand it on its own terms.

The value systems and atmospheres of schools reinforce the competitive classroom patterns of male dominance. Many teachers, particularly in elementary classrooms, often strive to create a homelike atmosphere. But the divisions among students, teachers, and administrators and the impersonality of school cultures run against the goals of people who would make schools more democratic and responsive to everyone in them. Schools are hierarchies, and the most responsible people in schools, the ones most connected to children, have the lowest status and are the most likely to be women: namely, the teachers. Teachers' connections to the children, one reason many go into teaching, are often sacrificed to the dictates of the administration and the local curriculum coordinator. Teachers are also isolated from each other. Moreover, school cultures also reinforce student hierarchies based on gender oppression: Football is often the highest status activity and the main public face of the high school, and sexual harassment among students is common and commonly ignored by adults. Teachers need more control over what and how they teach. They need time with each other to share their experiences, and they need some say in how the school functions as a whole.

Women-Centered Classrooms and Schools for Everyone

We argue that the curriculum content, learning styles and, above all, the relational values associated with women and their activities and experiences in the world should form a basis for rethinking our educational systems. When we look at the lives and perspectives of women, a new world of knowledge and creativity opens up to us, from the whole range of literary and artistic achievements, to a rich and complex history, to different perspectives on a number of issues. What were women's lives like on the frontier, as immigrants, as slaves? Did the prospect of leaving children behind restrain female slaves from running away? If girls are turning off of science in the second grade, could it be that they are not as enthusiastic about dinosaurs as boys are? What science topics would appeal to everyone? In the celebration of Thanksgiving, what were the different activities carried on by men and women in both cultures? Both sexes can learn the skills of home-making, just as both can learn woodworking. For many, sex equity seems to entail opening up boys' activities to girls, but boys have as much to learn as girls from encountering a wider world of human experience and from transcending traditional gender role limitations. Indeed, a curriculum built on human difference opens up cultural, racial, and ethnic diversities as well.

A women-centered approach goes way beyond curricula, however. Students have different learning styles, and female students in particular often benefit from working in collaborative groups and learning from each other. Girls are often more afraid of speaking up when they do not know "the right answer"; teachers need to encourage their more tentative explorations toward understanding. In the realms of science and math, some students, particularly girls, learn more from approaches that are concrete and grounded in real-world issues, rather than based on memorization of abstract principles, and again many boys would benefit from such methods. Belenky et al. (1986) discussed the role of the teacher as "midwife" and explained how teachers may practice "maternal thinking," in Sara Ruddick's terminology.

> In maternal thinking . . . the primary concern is the vulnerable child. The midwife–teacher's first concern is to preserve the students' fragile newborn thoughts, to see if they are born with the truth intact, that they do not turn into acceptable lies. . . . The second concern is to foster the child's growth. Connected teachers support the evolution of their children's thinking. . . . Midwife–teachers focus not on their own knowledge (as the lecturer does) but on the students' knowledge. (p. 218)

Another issue is teachers themselves. Teaching is a low-status and low-paying profession, as is the whole field of education, partially because most teachers are women. Underneath this, however, lies a deep societal contempt for activities, such as teaching and mothering, commonly associated with women. These qualities are deemed to be natural, intuitive, and inherently feminine, unlike masculine activities, which have to be "learned" and "mastered." In reality, teaching, like mothering, is a complex set of skills that must balance nurturing and encouragement with discernment and detachment. It is time to celebrate the inherent value of the work that teachers do, work that is women's work precisely *because* it is concerned fundamentally with children's growth as individuals.

Finally, it is time that our classrooms and schools recognized the inherent benefits, to our schools and to our whole society, of values and qualities long relegated to the private sphere and ignored as irrelevant to society's public activities. Feminist scholars such as Jane Roland Martin and

Nel Noddings have applied their theories of women's familial and relational orientation to school settings to argue that these values would help boys as well as girls grow and thrive in school. Nel Noddings has argued that schools and teachers should ground their approaches in caring relationships for children: "The teacher thinks with her students, placing at their bestowal the benefit of her knowledge, skill and sympathy" (quoted in Thompson, 1997, p. 327).

Jane Roland Martin (1985) has pointed out that schools prepare students only for the productive, and never for the reproductive, aspects of society. Schools teach children to learn, and sometimes to think, but not how to feel and respond to each other. In many classrooms, the rules are based on standards of fairness and equal treatment; few emphasize empathy and listening to one another. Schools teach children how to be public citizens but not necessarily how to be responsive members of families and communities. Martin wants teachers to build the qualities of the "3 Cs"— care, concern, and connection—into their curricula and classroom practices, and she wants teachers to work with each other to transform school cultures beyond the classroom. To conclude, whereas liberal feminists want to remove the barriers from women entering into the public sphere, women-centered feminists want to bring to the public sphere, and to the schools, a badly needed emphasis on the *connections* among people needed for democracies to thrive. Diversity can be valued only if all members of the community are fully heard and learn to care for one another.

Comments and Questions

"The Women-Centered View and You"

General Questions

1. What aspects of this viewpoint were appealing to you?
2. What aspects do you disagree with?
3. Do any aspects seem familiar from your knowledge of schooling, or, on the other hand, unrealistic in terms of today's schools?

Specific Questions

1. How does this viewpoint compare with the liberal-progressive view? What issues does it raise that liberals seem to ignore?

2. Conversely, about what issues does this viewpoint seem silent? How would the proponents of women-centered feminism deal with race, culture, and class differences among women? How about similarities to men?

3. What about academic standards? For example, doesn't making math and science "more accessible" to some students mean watering it down? What would teachers attached to this viewpoint do differently in their classrooms and their schools?

Again, we now return to the case studies and briefly analyze them according to the women-centered perspective. Do you think our analysis fits how people with this perspective would view each case? When you look at the specific case analyses that follows, do you agree with them or not? After thinking about these analyses, do you still feel the same way about the women-centered view?

"Sexism and the Classroom"

The proponents of the women-centered view would want to promote the values of caring, concern, and connection, thought of as women's virtues, throughout the curriculum and classroom practices. They would want Nina to have not only girls reading about boy heroes but also boys reading about girls. Nina should not only make sure that the girls are protected and represented, however; she should also work on transforming the whole atmosphere of the class. Women-centered teachers would be careful about setting up the whole classroom collaboratively and about getting the children to learn habits of responsibility and caring toward one another. They would be concerned not only about equity and fairness but also about building the classroom as a warm and supportive learning community.

"Gender, Race, and Teacher Expectations"

A woman-centered approach would emphasize the capacity of the teacher to build a supportive environment in which Charlie and other students like him could flourish. Such an approach would entail asking questions about the actions teachers can take in their classroom to reduce harmful competition and help the other students and Charlie to understand and care for each other. They would emphasize the development of collaborative groups and other changes in the atmosphere of the class to draw in students like Charlie. They would attend to how to build the classroom community relationships that would keep Charlie in the class. Beyond the classroom, they would advocate for policies that promote the most possible inclusion of special-needs students in the school community.

"Who Gets Hurt?"

A women-centered, feminist teacher would want Sarah to create a classroom policy of fairness and respect. Sarah should also emphasize the lives and experiences of women and gays in her curriculum materials. She should work on setting up support groups for gay, lesbian, and bisexual youth, to counter their low self-esteem, confusion, and isolation and to give them a community where they could be themselves. Sarah should also be concerned with the whole school culture. The school should adopt sexual harassment policies and other measures to enforce an atmosphere of acceptance and safety for all students. Women-centered teachers would want to sponsor assemblies and special events to promote diversity and to organize faculty and staff, as well as students, to support gay and lesbian students and teachers to feel at ease and safe about being "out."

"A Woman's Career?"

Women-centered feminists would want Helen, whatever path she chose, to keep gender issues in mind—either to focus on women's health in her science career, for example, or to make gender issues and her female pupils a special concern in her teaching. Women-centered advocates might also want Helen to use the water unit to look at the gender relations in the life of the community. In her classroom, she should pay particular attention to the girls in relation to science topics and make sure her teaching techniques and curriculum interventions are designed to enhance their participation.

A "RADICAL-MULTICULTURAL VIEW": GENDER, CULTURE, AND SOCIETAL TRANSFORMATION

Introduction

The most important challenge teachers face today is to reach children in terms of this basic understanding: that all children have gender, race, cultural, and class positions; that they live in cultural contexts; and that these contexts are shaped by societal dynamics of power and privilege. Teachers must engage with their pupils, not only as individuals but also as people with gender, racial, class, *and* cultural identities. They must build democratic classroom communities that are grounded in these diversities as well as emphasize high standards of academic performance. Many of us are taught to treat children as individuals first, and this is very important. But a focus on individual potential may obscure the important cultural and societal sources of many children's relationships to school cultures and demands. On the other hand, many advocates of multicultural approaches ignore gender to focus on race or cultural issues, treating girls and boys from the same culture as a single unit, whereas feminists, emphasizing gender, ignore other differences. We think teachers ought to engage with the whole child, build democratic classroom communities based on the perspectives the children offer, and confront societal inequalities to help their pupils envision a more just and equitable society. And indeed, many educators have described how such approaches can be used in the classroom (see Adams et al., 1997; Bigelow et al., 1994; Levine, Lowe, Peterson, & Tenorio, 1995).

Our position is in direct opposition to the conservative one. Conservatives think that the problems in our society are caused by its victims, namely our most impoverished members. Therefore, they lay the blame for poor public schools on the children themselves. They say schools should be emphasizing the basics and "high standards," measured by standardized tests that judge everyone by a White, middle-class, male yardstick. As for gender equality, they think that feminists' demands for equality would ruin the family. They criticize non-European races and cultures for their refusal to assimilate to the American way. They want to preserve the economic and political status quo, whereas we want to change it.

However, we also disagree with major aspects of the liberal position. Like ourselves, liberals want a more equitable society, where the so-called "playing field" is made level for all. They are concerned with the ways in which families and schools engage in sex role stereotyping at early ages, because stereotypes interfere with girls and boys reaching their full potential. But liberal and progressive educators focus too much on individual children and teachers. They downplay gender differences, think the problem is mainly about stereotypes, and ignore the sex-based power arrangements on which gender difference and inequality rest.

Women-centered theorists are concerned with women's oppression and gender difference in ways that liberals are not, but they ignore differences based on race, class, and culture, as feminists of color such as bel hooks and Patricia Hill Collins have pointed out (see hooks, 1989, and Collins, 1990). We think diversities of gender, race, and class *must* be addressed in the classroom and connected to issues in the wider community.

Indeed, schools and classrooms are great places where children can learn about the demands and possibilities of living in a democratic society. Although many of our classrooms and schools are all too homogeneous, given the social class and racial segregation of so many of our communities, almost all educational settings represent some varieties, of gender at least. Teachers working with girls and boys, even from different neighborhoods, can start with the children's lived lives, exploring how they intersect and how children may learn from each other. And every teacher ought to go beyond his or her classroom to introduce students to the richness of other cultures in this country, as many writers on multicultural education have shown (see our Bibliography, especially Bigelow et al., 1994; Grant & Sleeter, 1989; and Schniedewind & Davidson, 1998). Every teacher can use his or her classroom to address the dynamics of power and privilege in our society, including racism, sexism, and homophobia (Adams et al., 1997; Logan, 1993; Wheeler, 1993). Teaching about differences of all kinds ought to inform one another; indeed, in order to teach well, teachers *must* relate to the cultural and gendered features of children's lives.

Some Essential Facts

At no time in American history has there been such a gap between the rich and the poor. Most of these are the "working poor," not the prototypical women on welfare. They are poor because most blue-collar jobs are in the low-paying service sector of our economy. Families need two and three incomes to make ends meet, so that women have to work; it is low wages, rather than feminism, that take women away from home and children and threaten our so-called "family values." In the educational arena we face disintegrating public schools in many communities, a loss of public money and support for public education, and a burgeoning charter school movement that is threatening to privatize our public school system and pit different groups of teachers, parents, and children against each other. As documented by Jonathan Kozol (1992) and others, community and state funding to support public schools adequately is notoriously lacking, often because of property tax inequities. Yet the groups blamed are often women, such as poor women of color who have too many children, female teachers who don't know how to teach, and working mothers who spend too little time with their children.

Schools, indeed, are places where such prejudices are nurtured. Teachers, themselves derided in the public consciousness, are encouraged to see many children as primed for failure; little boys like Charlie who act up are cast as future gang members, the girls as future teenage mothers. Through their tracking systems and other practices, schools reinforce rather than challenge long-standing social class, race, and gender hierarchies (Spring, 2000). Such scapegoating conceals the fact that it is not the children's or teachers' fault that schools are falling apart. The educational status quo rewards only competition and individual achievement, ignores the societal context that explains the persistence and growth of inequality, and blames the hardest-hit victims of poor schooling for their educational failures. We need schools that get appropriate resources and where teachers are trained to teach *all* the children. Schools in a democracy should prepare students in every kind of setting to work on solving these problems.

Our Plan for Transformation

What do we propose? We want our schools to produce boys and girls, men and women, who are safe, self-confident, and able to see themselves as both potentially successful and responsible for making a difference in the world. For this we need pedagogies and curricula that "center" all children, not just those in the mainstream. Teachers, their instructional practices, and the curriculum materials they use must engage with gender differences, as informed by culturally specific gender dynamics, in order to educate children to understand and celebrate themselves and others. To these ends, teachers must be culture- and gender-sensitive and be open to all forms of diversity. They must be aware of their own journeys, their own struggles, and their own limitations as gendered, raced, and classed members of our society. As one of our respondents put it, "It is important to understand our own journey, beliefs, level of sexist (and racist and homophobic) awareness, and our sense of who we are in the world as we turn around to teach children to understand themselves as well."

Teachers need tools for practicing classroom democracy in an atmosphere of sensitivity to gender and cultural differences. Although children's feelings are important, democracy is not just about letting kids express themselves but realizing, as in several of our cases, that some students' behaviors may be unfair to some and may silence others. Teachers need to establish classroom practices and pedagogies of respect and encouragement for all pupils. They need to think not only about their children as individuals but also about how to integrate issues of gender, race, class, and culture as they intersect in children's lives. Curriculum materials should analyze societal inequalities as reflected in gender, race, and class dynamics. Curricula should reflect the fact that cultural locations and psychological identities are different for boys and girls within any culture and different across cultures as well. We need curricula that center all children, enabling them to see themselves reflected in what they learn. Rather than relying solely on standardized tests, assessments should be multiple and various, including portfolios and other examples of students' original work. Assessments should reflect the best of what pupils can do and capture the variety of their talents and achievements in a number of areas.

At present, many school subjects are gender-, race-, and class-segregated, reflecting and reinforcing societal status hierarchies. In the case of mathematics, for example, women and members of racial minority groups are routinely assumed to be incapable of and uninterested in the kind of advanced work that is a prerequisite for many prestigious occupations. We believe that all students should have access to all types of subjects, so that girls should be encouraged in math and science and boys in English and foreign languages. In each of these areas, pedagogies and curriculum materials should be designed to incorporate students' varying learning styles and interests so that these subjects will become relevant and attractive to all students.

Both inside and outside the classroom, we think that teachers should help their students understand how gender structures kids' lives in all areas of school. As educators we need to take on the hidden curricula of gender differences and sexism in the broader school culture. We need to understand that kids reflect and reproduce the gender and racial–cultural roles they learn through family, school, and the culture at large. We need to take on such issues as the toleration of sexual harassment and homophobia, the valorization of traditional masculinities and femininities in the guise of football and cheerleading, and the way gender and other stereotypes structure school life and limit kids' potential. Indeed, a power analysis of these dynamics could be central to the curriculum. How do gender differences provide a template and a justification for other forms of inequality? How do race and gender stereotypes intersect, so that White girls' passivity is set against the supposed aggressiveness of Black girls and all boys? By forcing all kids to deal with such expectations as they negotiate their identities, such prejudices limit all children's potential.

CONCLUSION

Differences of gender, race, class, and culture should be understood as bases for the strength and vitality of any culture and any community. In our schools today, they represent differential positions in societal hierarchies of inequality. They are used as excuses for why children don't do well, and they form the bases for hierarchies within the school, whether in terms of the tracking system or the grounds for popularity on the playground. Thus schools reinforce inequalities and provide excuses for them, through a rhetoric of competition and achievement that says success is only up to the individual.

This situation has to change. Schools and teachers must begin to center children in curricula, pedagogies, and school cultures. Within the school, teachers, students, and administrators can work for reforms such as detracking and heterogeneous grouping, as well as setting up committees devoted to multiracial and anti-homophobia training and other initiatives (see Oakes, 1985; Wheelock, 1992). Moreover, schools based on such principles can also begin to reach out to parents and citizens in the wider community, who can then begin to see the schools as centers for community building and renewal. Administrations, school boards, and social welfare agencies in the wider community should take responsibility for rejuvenating interest and support in our public schools, beginning with pushing for equal district funding at the state level. Our schools can be places where students learn to understand and value our tremendous range of gender, race, and cultural perspectives. They can not only give students practice in creating a truly multicultural democracy but also equip them to envision larger social changes and work for social justice.

Comments and Questions

"The Radical-Multicultural View and You"

General Questions

1. What aspects of this viewpoint were appealing to you?
2. What aspects do you disagree with?
3. Do any aspects seem familiar from your knowledge of schooling, or, on the other hand, unrealistic in terms of today's schools?

Specific Questions

1. How does this viewpoint compare with the liberal-progressive and women-centered views? What issues does it raise that these views seem to ignore?
2. Conversely, about what issues does this viewpoint seem silent? Is there enough attention to the specifics of gender differences and to women's special qualities and strengths? Doesn't this viewpoint ignore all the progress that has been made in terms of gender equity and cultural diversity?
3. What about academic standards? How can a curriculum be culture- and gender-sensitive and still prepare all students to meet common high academic expectations?
4. What would teachers attached to this viewpoint do differently in their classrooms and their schools?

Again, we now return to the case studies and begin briefly to analyze them according to the radical-multicultural perspective. Do you think our analysis fits how people with this perspective would view each case? When you look at the specific case analyses that follow, do you agree with them or not? After thinking about these analyses, do you still feel the same way about this viewpoint?

"Sexism and the Classroom"

Like women-centered teachers, radical-multicultural teachers would be concerned about equity and caring and would see it as important to call on all children equally and to create collaborative classroom arrangements. However, they would want to locate gender inequity within a larger constellation of societal inequalities. They would see gender, race, class, and culture as interlocking categories of discrimination, oppression, and potential empowerment. Students would learn from all kinds of people in all types of communities doing all manner of different things, including traditionally female and male activities. Gender differences would be downplayed in the arrangement of classroom seats, the lines to the bathroom, the assignments of classroom duties, and so on. A variety of family forms might be looked at and celebrated, so that the traditional family becomes only one model. The curriculum would be organized around social and community issues, and readings and activities would emphasize the activist roles of both women and men.

"Gender, Race, and Teacher Expectations"

Radical-multicultural teachers would attend to a number of issues raised in this case. They would identify Charlie's situation in this school as exemplifying a whole culture of exclusionary practices encompassing a set of subjective and highly questionable beliefs about sorting, ranking, and categorizing students. Race and gender relationships raised in this case and the problems that arise in cross-racial interactions would also elicit concern. The examination of the relationships between White women who are teachers and other teachers of color, as well as between White teachers and male students of color, show the importance of the intersection of race and gender dynamics in the classroom. Such teachers would view these relationships as sites of contestation and opportunities for intervention. Multicultural educators would attend to the need to sensitize classroom teachers, special-education specialists, and administrators to cultural differences in their student body, introducing programs designed to overcome the lack of accurate information about low-income minority populations in particular. Current data on the effects of specific educational practices on non-White children would be critically examined and shared with other educators in the hope of avoiding the damaging effects of poor practices. They would familiarize themselves with models for working with diverse student populations that highlight best classroom instruction and behavior management practices for all children. Standardized testing would probably raise a number of questions for these educators. Because culture and gender bias concerns them deeply, these educators would need to be assured that when standardized tests are used they have been normed on appropriate populations, with questions drawn from, and familiar to, the students tested. These educators would probably prefer the adoption of alternative assessment techniques, such as portfolio assessment and "authentic assessment."

"Who Gets Hurt?"

Radical-multicultural teachers would make sure that general course themes of oppression, resistance, and societal power relations included sexuality as well as gender, race, and class, emphasizing the interconnectedness of all these social issues. Outside the classroom, they would be in favor of support groups for gay, lesbian, and bisexual youth, realizing that much of gay and lesbian students' oppression occurs outside of the classroom. Also, they would push for the establishment of adequate and enforceable sexual harassment policies. They would want to organize faculty and staff, as well as students, to support gay and lesbian students and teachers to feel comfortable and safe about being "out."

However, for them the issue would be larger than the marginalization of only gay and lesbian students. They would emphasize schoolwide curricular and extracurricular interventions to create a more open and accepting community for everyone. Rather than accepting a sexist, racist, or homophobic peer culture, they would want to challenge their school and school system to adopt measures to enforce an atmosphere of acceptance and safety for all students. To this end, they would want Sarah and her colleagues not only to protect marginalized students but also to confront the football team and the school practices and policies that valorize them. Sarah should work for a school built around the positive celebration of all kinds of diversity and figure out how to examine and challenge the oppressive power relations that hinder all marginalized groups from thriving in school.

"A Woman's Career?"

Advocates such as Helen's professor, Jane Dexter, would see the chance for Helen, in becoming a teacher, to be a real change agent in her classroom and school and to make a direct difference in her pupils' lives and in the life of the school community. They would argue that such teachers are rare, unfortunately, and always sorely needed. Helen should examine the whole range of power relations between the dominant culture and groups marginalized by culture, race, gender, and class discrimination. Proponents of this view would ask what Helen needs to know about the communities her students are from, and about herself, as a White person, when she prepares to work with students different from her. She must learn to think about her own position as a representative of the dominant culture, as she simultaneously learns more about theirs. Finally, proponents of the radical-multicultural position would locate the students' progress in science within a wider project of understanding the ways in which the dominant culture has historically locked marginalized groups out of science and math. Programs such as Robert Moses's Algebra Project help African American and working-class middle schoolers learn algebra through the mobilization of teachers and parents throughout entire schools (Moses et al., 1989). This is a political as well as an educational issue, demanding conscious organization of the resources of the community, because mastery of algebraic skills means access to college-track courses and a whole range of future careers commonly denied working-class students and students of color as well as young women.

The issues in this case are not black and white; rather, the case is meant to illustrate the need for female teachers in particular to reflect on the ways they think they can "make a difference" with students and with a community. The case directly attacks the idea that simply "loving children" and "settling for" teaching over "a real career" can be a basis for this career choice. There is no other career that more effectively combines intellectual, social, and moral choices and responsibilities and no other that calls for more reflection—both at the point of entry and all the way through.

III

FINAL ARGUMENTS, AND SOME SUGGESTIONS AND RESOURCES FOR FURTHER REFLECTION

THE CENTRALITY OF GENDER FOR REFLECTIVE TEACHING AND LEARNING: UNDERSTANDING THE INTERPLAY OF GENDER, RACE, CLASS, AND CULTURE IN EDUCATIONAL SETTINGS

In this final section we accomplish three tasks. We present briefly the main elements of our own considered points of view in terms of the public arguments you have just read. We outline some activities and questions that should help you think further about the issues raised so far. Finally, we provide an annotated bibliography that should provide resources for discussion, reflection, and your own research. Most teachers obviously find valuable features in all four of the public arguments we have offered. Indeed, most of us, including teachers, carry around complex and even contradictory views about children, about schooling, and most particularly about gender issues. One of the most difficult aspects of our thinking about gender, especially, is that much of what we think and do comes from largely unconscious assumptions about ourselves, our gender, and what is appropriate for men and women, boys and girls. Yet all of us—the authors, our respondents, our readers, and teachers everywhere—act on both conscious and unconscious ideas when we make decisions in classrooms, in schools, and in our own lives. We have chosen our cases, their responses, and our public arguments partly to try to examine and uncover some of these ideas that we usually assume without thinking what they might mean to ourselves and others.

Our own perspective may be summed up by saying that we believe in a radical social reconstructionist view, probably most like the radical-multicultural view elaborated in Part II, with admixtures of all the others. Our main concern is the manner in which larger cultural, social, and political dynamics, in classrooms, in schools, and in the wider society harm and distort the education we offer our children, particularly children of color and working-class and poor children. Unlike many writers from this critical reconstructionist perspective, however, we think that gender, too, is a tool for enforcing varieties of inequalities in schools. Gender interacts with and often exacerbates the other forms of discrimination and silencing that many children face, and gender discrimination and prejudices hurt everyone. We want to foster educational settings that reflect and promote the shared and distinct understandings of people from varied backgrounds. This means different gender positions as well: gays and lesbians as well as heterosexual pupils and teachers.

There are several reasons for articulating our own views in this way. Because we put this text together we thought we owed you a more direct and complete presentation of our own perspectives and assumptions. You should know where authors—all authors—stand. Because we believe it is important for you to begin to articulate your own viewpoint, we offer our understandings as one way to think about the issues of gender and teaching. Our views—like everyone's, we hope—are evolving and changing and are by no means identical to each other's. Although working together on this book would not have been possible had we not deeply agreed in our basic orientations, we nevertheless also have different experiences of and perspectives on all these issues, Janie as an African American educator, and Frances as a European American one. This volume is part of our ongoing and evolving conversation with each other about these matters.

Another way to think further about the issues outlined in this volume is to inquire into the world around you. Visits to classrooms, playgrounds, and athletic fields—anywhere you can see girls and boys living their lives; or observations in courts, school board meetings, and social service agencies; or analyses of the media and texts: All such explorations can reveal aspects of the gendered, raced, classed, and cultured world in which we live. We next outline some activities in the hopes that you will be encouraged to try some, inquire, and reflect further.

Education Through the Lenses of Gender

The issues raised by the intermingling of gender, cultural, and racial–ethnic issues with education and schooling seem to lack any simple or ready solutions. Numerous questions come to mind. How does one create a more equitable and just educational system in a society that we believe is essentially inequitable and unjust? How does one openly explore inequalities in the classroom when these inequalities will put some children at a persistent disadvantage? For example, how can a teacher emphasize the importance of including materials by women without admitting that most history and literature books have been about, and been written by, privileged men? What should all students experience that is part of our common culture, if anything, and how can such commonalities be arrived at in a society as divided and unequal as ours is today?

It is true that education is behind almost every success story in this society, from the tales of the immigrants in the last century to the increasing numbers of students, especially women, who are making it to college today. At the same time, however, a lot of research has shown that, rather than being agencies for promoting social equality, schools instead tend to reinforce, exacerbate, and provide an official justification for the very inequalities they are supposed to overcome. Whether through the overt or the hidden curriculum, traditional gender, race, and class stereotypes prevail. It is the very pervasiveness of these stereotypes and assumptions that allow people to think of them as desirable and "the norm." People like Frank, Charlie, or the female students in Nina's and Helen's classes are the victims. If we began looking at schooling through the lenses of gender awareness, coupled with attentiveness to race, ethnic, and cultural factors, we could see schools in a completely different way. Sexist assumptions and practices, enforced by gender differences and gender expectations, shape the ways we think about our schools, our teachers, and our children in schools, and some of these assumptions need to change.

Gender, Teaching, and Teachers

First, what would happen to our ideas and hopes about schools and classrooms if we understood the multiple significance of the fact that most teachers are women and that, furthermore, the *idea* of the teacher in our society is that she is a woman? (About 80% of our elementary teachers are women, about 50% of high school teachers are women, and the majority of school administrators are men.) In the first place, we could begin to see why teachers are poorly paid and devalued by most people. After all, teaching is a women's profession, like nursing and, of course, mothering. Many people believe, without even realizing that they hold this belief, that teaching is easy and comes naturally to women because of their inborn capacities for caretaking and nurturance. Therefore, the training that they need is minimal, and the pay they deserve is the same. Indeed, the only real kind of training teachers *need* is in their subject matter (the rest is innate). So college professors, who are of course teachers as well (and are mostly male) are respected for what they know, not for how well they convey it. One author commented:

> Most accounts of the "good teacher" [don't take account of any idea of] professionalism at both ends of the spectrum: the scholar, because his calling is based on his own gifts and passion for the subject; the mother/teacher, because in her own way she is doing what comes naturally. It is also remarkable that both extremes of the "good teacher" make any sort of [pedagogical] training appear unnecessary. (Miller, 1996, pp. 106–107)

In other words, good teachers are either experts in their field who know their subject matter, which is what males who dominate the upper grades and colleges are noted for, or kindly nurturers, which is what women who dominate the younger grades are noted for.

What are some results of this kind of thinking on our teachers and our schools? You may be wondering how some people's prejudices and lack of understanding of how demanding teaching is, intellectually as well as socially and psychologically, could actually affect educational policy. Surely the people who are in charge of schools know better! But consider the following.

1. Education courses are looked down on by other faculty, students, and departments, and degrees in education are seen as second-class degrees.
2. In many schools, the curricula and even the pedagogies are determined not by the teachers but by districts and curriculum coordinators. Teachers are not presumed to be knowledgeable and skilled enough to plan curricula on their own.
3. Chances are high these days you will have to take a teacher test to be certified. Although in many states the teacher test has items on pedagogical issues, in many others *only* subject matter knowledge is tested. People with no training in education whatsoever are being recruited and certified as long as they can pass a subject matter test only.
4. Teachers are the least well paid of any professional group, and none of the current reform initiatives is addressing this issue.

Perhaps most harmful of all is that if teachers were supported and respected for the work they do then there might be more attention given to the actual challenges they face in schools. The shocking conditions in urban schools might come into view: the persisting patterns of segregation (both between schools and within schools because of the tracking system), sharply unequal funding, burgeoning class sizes, and inferior materials and equipment. Indeed, this emphasis on teacher testing as the main facet of today's "education reform" initiatives might lead one to think that education reform is not about what schools really need; it is about blaming teachers, who are mostly female, for the failures in our schools. The result of these kinds of prejudices and policies is that teachers are not given the support and the training they need to function as thoughtful and autonomous experts in helping all their students learn. To see teachers as "transformative intellectuals," as the educator Henry Giroux (1998) put it, is to begin to see how they can bring the necessary combination of intellectual rigor, culturally relevant knowledge, and personal sensitivity to all their pupils.

Who Is a Good Teacher?

Fortunately, however, there are many, many teachers, as you know, who have transcended the limitations of the ways that their job has been defined and the ways that the public has been taught to view what they do. It is central to our perspective to emphasize that in spite of the odds, good teachers in all kinds of classrooms, all over our country, are making successful learning communities for all their students. Such teachers emphasize not only academic rigor but also the need for supportive classroom communities where everyone is at home and has something to gain and to give. They also help their children understand the need to work to make our society a better and more equal place: Such teachers have a strong social justice agenda. Indeed, for teachers of children of color and working-class children, these three goals are interdependent: To foster academic achievement is to overturn the overwhelming societal odds against their children.

Let us think again in this context about the qualities associated with women and female teachers, such as caring, nurturing, and the fostering of supportive learning communities. It becomes clear that these qualities and practices are in fact extremely important, but *not* because they are natural and instinctive; caring must be learned. And they are not "soft," not the "opposite" of, or at another extreme from, academic rigor. Rather, they are a central quality of a demanding and successful teacher, whether male or female. As Deborah Meier, a prominent education reformer, put it:

Care and compassion are not soft, mushy goals. They are part of the hard core of subjects we are responsible for teaching. Informed and skillful care is learned. Caring is as much cognitive as effective. The capacity to see the world as others might is central to unsentimental compassion and at the root of both intellectual skepticism and empathy. . . . Empathetic qualities are precisely the habits of mind that require deliberate cultivation—that is, schooling. If such habits are central to democratic life, our schools must become places that cultivate, consciously and rigorously, these moral and intellectual fundamentals. (Meier, 1995, p. 63)

Although critics have often distorted their messages as an exclusively woman's viewpoint, feminist authors such as Carol Gilligan, Mary Belenky, Nel Noddings, and Jane Roland Martin have all argued forcefully for education in just these qualities and ways of knowing in our schools and in the conduct of our public life.

In the next section of our perspective-taking we discuss briefly what kinds of approaches such successful teachers build, but before we do that we first urge you to read one or more of a number of books that focus on successful teachers. These books will not only give you a good sense of how many and varied they are but also help you learn from their methods, materials and approaches, and their mistakes! The books in the Bibliography by Judy Logan, Mike Rose, Gloria Ladson-Billings, Michelle Foster, Carla Rensenbrink, and Kathleen Weiler are all portraits of such teachers.

What are the approaches that these teachers share? In spite of their differences—and they are female and male, Black and White, elementary and secondary, urban and suburban and rural, experienced and young—they all firmly believe, in the words of Tamara Beauboeuf-Lafontant (1999), "that formal education has a responsibility to prepare students to take an active role in making society truly democratic" (pp. 703–704). It is probably no coincidence that many of the teachers described in these books are African American women. As Beauboeuf-Lafontant explained in her article on African American female teachers, what is necessary is "politically relevant teaching":

Because of the political understanding of education held by these educators, their actions are sensitive to and supportive of the anti-racism and anti-oppression struggles of students of color generally. . . . In other words, regardless of their culture of origin, culturally relevant teachers appear to share an understanding of systemic inequality—that is, the political, economic and racial structures that disproportionately limit the opportunities of children of color. (Beauboeuf-Lafontant, 1999, p. 704)

We believe that this model may fit any teachers who help their children understand the unequal power relationships in our society, which privilege some students (such as Whites, middle-class children, and males) at the expense of others and use their classrooms as laboratories to name, challenge, and change these dynamics by looking at them directly. For White children this means introducing the idea of White privilege and the responsibilities and challenges that go along with this. All teachers can learn from how the African American female teachers in the traditionally Black segregated schools that Beauboeuf-Lafontant described worked with their pupils.

> When teachers from the former County Training School talk about their students and their day-to-day interactions with them, they frequently described . . . how they wanted to "make the children believe they were somebody." . . . This caring that the students perceived to be at the root of their interactions with the teachers made them feel they could relate to the teachers, made them want to be like their teachers, and made them believe what the teachers told them about their potential for success. (Beauboeuf-Lafontant, 1999, p. 711)

These comments resonate with the work of many others as well. Carla Rensenbrink included the following teacher, a White woman, in her study of three feminist elementary school teachers. She, too, worked to make her classroom hospitable to diversity by insisting on challenging the societal inequalities and prejudices behind gender, heterosexual, and racial privilege. This teacher told Carla:

> Gender roles have to break down—you know, girls don't have to be a certain way, boys don't have to be a certain way . . . in terms of gender roles, never mind of homophobia, that there are a million little suicides that can happen, you know, like when boys say, "I can't join chorus because I am a boy." (Rensenbrink, 2000, p. 156)

Rensenbrink added,

> [This teacher] worked to deal with the gender differences in her classroom by controlling the atmosphere in which these differences played out. Working towards a society in which "It's ok to be who you are," she insists that the children in her class deal with and learn from each other's differences. She keeps that conversation going. She works to empower her students so that they can take their place and speak their mind. (2000, p. 173)

We have included these quotes to show how successful teachers, whether male or female, combine an ethic of care and a rigorous attention to academic excellence with a commitment to diversity in the name of challenging societal inequalities. We think sexist and racist prejudices against teachers obscure and distort the work they do, allowing schools to further deteriorate and making the obstacles they face that much greater.

Girls and Boys in Classrooms

How do such teachers accomplish their goals? We now turn to some important features of the classroom communities that such teachers create for their students. In the first place, teachers need to be aware of and knowledgeable about their own and their students' gender and cultural identities and assumptions. This includes a keen and informed understanding of their own race and gender positions and the likelihood that, as middle-class professionals, they inhabit a privileged status in relation to many of their students. Teachers should also become deeply familiar with the communities their children come from—their parents, their neighborhoods, and the role of the school in the community. Beauboeuf-Lafontant remarked of the teachers she studied:

> These educators became part of students' extended families, as they resided, worshipped and worked in the same communities as their students.
> . . . Black teachers were able to create home-like atmospheres in schools, where students experienced a continuity of expectations and interactional patterns between their homes and schools, their parents and their teachers.
> (p. 710)

Looking back on our cases, we see that community and school awareness and knowledge could be an important factor in our teachers' approaches to solving their dilemmas. Nina should learn how the parents of her class as well as their Hispanic community feel about the issues that come up in her class; she cannot assume that because she too is Hispanic that she knows what they think and feel. Amy could find out about Charlie's family and the larger context of how Black children are viewed and treated in her school. Both Helen and Amy must learn to take account of their own racial privilege. Sarah should take some measure of community attitudes and learn about the role of the high school in the town. And all of them need to find allies among their colleagues, to break down the isolation that they, along with many other classroom teachers, face.

How about inside the classroom? We agree with the conservative position that schools must pay attention to character development and citizenship, but we see it in a different way. To us citizenship is about teaching to build a democratic society, which we do not yet have, not about blind loyalty to a common culture based on the viewpoints of the privileged. Character development is about helping all children respect each other's differences and contributions, both personal and cultural, in the context of caring and supportive classroom communities. This kind of teaching is not a blind acceptance of student differences, the kind that simply makes sure that all cultures are represented on Thanksgiving Day or allows children to act out because "boys will be boys." Teachers must also work to challenge the societal inequalities that operate in each and every classroom, because they operate in the culture. Teachers who are social reconstructionists make sure the curriculum contains explicit references to inequality and resistance.

For example, Thanksgiving may become an occasion not to exoticize Indian culture but to explore the historical record in all its complexities and present-day political struggles. As for gender differences, an example might be Judy Logan, whom we quoted earlier, whose proactive approach enlists both boys and girls in a consideration of what gender identities and differences might mean to them. One day, she had the students close their eyes and had them imagine *being* the other gender, with all its benefits and burdens. In the discussion, she told the girls to listen to the boys, and vice versa, so that "we can begin to understand what they think being female (or male) is all about." For a project on Women's History Month, Logan's students all studied a woman's life, choosing from a wide diversity of women from many cultures, including family members. They could choose any woman but they did have to choose a woman (Logan, 1993, pp. 10, 22–24). One of the teachers Carla Rensenbrink studied helps her class design and carry out social action projects, based on newspaper articles discussed in their daily current events lesson. As in Helen's water unit, they learn to pursue their learning outside the classroom. In these examples, the teachers do not simply allow diverse viewpoints to flourish; they build diversity and the social analyses necessary to understand the power relations of various forms of diversity into their curricula from the start.

The dilemmas faced by the teachers in our case studies are common issues in such classrooms, where social and cultural differences are not swept under the table or repressed but in fact are confronted and dealt with. Feminist teachers who are social reconstructionists would make such crises part of ongoing journeys of exploration with their students. To quote Judy Logan (1993) again:

In each class, I have children with a diversity of interests, abilities, talents and learning styles. . . . When I think of curriculum, I think of a journey. In traditional curriculum, everyone is supposed to be on the same journey at the same time, and the teacher's role is like that of a sheep dog, trying to keep everyone together. . . . And I think of feminist curriculum as a journey that acknowledges that while everyone needs to be moving forward, most of us are in different places at different times.

Some people are filling out passport applications; some people are touring beautiful cathedrals and famous monuments; some people are sitting in cafes having bread and cheese and intense conversations; some people are learning Japanese; some are homesick, writing letters home; some are putting together their photo albums. The teacher's role in this vision becomes one of keen observer. After all, it is inappropriate to speak Japanese to someone who is filling out a passport application, and it is inappropriate to hand a photo album to someone eating and visiting in a cafe. (p. 45)

This implies that the football players in Sarah's class, no less than Holly and Frank, needed to understand the significance of their social position and privilege, and it is part of her responsibility to find some tools for them to do so.

If we didn't know about such teachers as Judy Logan, and all the teachers that Beauboeuf-Lafontant and others write about, we would think that our perspective was an unrealistic and utopian one. As it is, we know how difficult it is to teach in this way but also how difficult and costly it is to teach as if sexism, racism, and other forms of prejudice and unequal treatment did not exist. In spite of today's barriers and obstacles, we still think that it is in the classrooms of individual teachers, helped by allies in their schools and communities, that our best hopes for building democracy lie.

EXERCISES FOR FURTHER REFLECTION

In the paragraphs that follow we have tried to supplement our written text with suggestions for different kinds of learning experiences, ones that might facilitate further reflections on gender and teaching. All of the following exercises involve your powers of observation as well as interpretation. Many people who look at children, classrooms, and other situations, whether for the first time or with long association, react and judge on the basis of an immediate appraisal. Maybe this is especially true in classrooms, because unlike, say, a juvenile court, all of us have been in classrooms, at least as students. So it is easy to think that this scene is familiar, that we know "what is going on." Similarly, if we look at boys and girls interacting, we often think we "get" the scene in front of us; we may see a little boy grab a toy from a girl and say to ourselves, "Aha! There goes masculine aggression!" But maybe the little girl had snatched the toy away from him the minute before, when our backs were turned.

Although we are not going to suggest that you can observe without having reactions, we do want to suggest that you find ways to record what you are seeing as objectively as possible, including your own responses at the time, in such a way that you can return to your initial experiences later. This is what being a reflective and thoughtful observer is about, and it is a key feature of becoming a thoughtful and self-aware teacher. What is important here is to learn how to disentangle our own interpretations from what we are seeing and the feelings we are having. Other interpretations always exist for the scenes we observe and the experiences we encounter. Try to jot down notes on what you are seeing, and when you have noticeable personal reactions, questions, or interpretations, jot those down separately. Then, later, you can react to both the events and your initial responses.

Second, the best way to observe any setting is to settle down in it a bit rather than just "traveling through." School observations, including those on playgrounds and sports fields, can be combined with practicum time in schools. In some other places it might be best to become a volunteer, if that is possible, if only for 12–16 hrs during the semester. We hope you will be able to spend some time attempting to understand people and settings very different from your own. Finally, take these suggestions as just the beginning and think of places and questions you can explore by yourself.

Classroom Settings

Who talks and who doesn't? Find or design a coding scheme (many are available) to mark the frequency of children's responses; it is very hard to get the actual amount of talking right unless you have some kind of coding system. Think of some questions to ask about girls' and boys' behavior, including the degree of their interaction with each other. What questions can you ask about the teacher's behavior? Who has special needs, and how are they treated? Finally, examine the curriculum materials, the texts, and the classroom walls for evidence of gender, cultural, and racial awareness.

School Settings

Observe patterns of gender, race, and class interactions in classrooms, in the cafeteria, on the corridors. Who "hangs" with whom? How are children treated by each other? Do you see harassment? Bullying? Cliques? In spaces where children are allowed to interact more or less freely, what roles do adults play? Try to observe the same groups of children in different settings to see if their behavior changes. Make sure you look at boys and girls, White kids and kids of color. Can you tell anything about social class differences among the students? What are the grounds for becoming a member of the "popular" crowd? What happens to students like Charlie at recess? Make up your own questions. It is key to make your observations over a period of time, not just 1 day, so that you can see patterns emerging.

Community Settings

Go to sports practices, Little League and soccer games, for both genders. Make an observation form for player–player interactions and coach and parent interventions. Compare girls' and boys' sports; different age groups; and urban, suburban, and rural settings. What are the commonalities and differences? Pick a sport you play or used to play; this will help you understand better what is going on. Go to a local mall and watch the scene. Pick a few kids to follow. Where do they go, what do they buy, what do they talk about, how big are their groups? Do their activities vary by age, by race, by gender?

Community Organizations

There are of course many community organizations, from halfway houses, homeless shelters, and battered women's shelters to school boards and branches of the juvenile court system. Volunteer work in a battered women's shelter will teach you more about gender relations than many books on domestic violence. Visits to the school board and juvenile court will show you how policies toward young people are carried out. It is important before you visit a school board meeting or a courtroom that you understand the procedures followed; if you go to a school board meeting or meetings, familiarize yourself with the topics under consideration beforehand.

CONCLUSION

People "do" or "perform" gender, as well as race, class, culture, and many other aspects of their identity, in every waking moment. Many of the identities that people inhabit are ignored, demeaned, and stereotyped by the operations of our culture on their lives, their opportunities, and their sense of themselves as people. Schools are a crucial place for the development of knowledge, character, and citizenship in all our children, and it is up to our teachers to engage in the "politically relevant" pedagogies to help them thrive. We hope that this book has helped you to think about these issues in your own life—as a family and community member, as a citizen, and as a teacher—and to maintain a commitment to all students' learning.

BIBLIOGRAPHY

The following list includes both works referred to in the text and additional articles and books we thought might be beneficial. We have arranged our suggestions by category and have tried to keep the list manageable and short. Works marked with an * are those that are cited in this volume.

General Texts on Education, Women, and Women's Education

*Belenky, M., Clinchy, B., Goldberger, N., & Tarule, J. (1986). *Women's ways of knowing: The development of self, body and mind.* New York: Basic Books. The classic work on women's different and unique ways of learning, epistemologies, and outlooks on education. Articulates a model of "connected" as opposed to separate knowing.

*Chodorow, N. (1999). *The reproduction of mothering: Psychoanalysis and the sociology of gender* (2nd ed.). Berkeley: University of California Press. How women's roles as mothers shape their psyches and help create daughters who themselves "mother." A feminist view of Freudian theory.

Collins, P. H. (1990). *Black feminist thought: Knowledge, consciousness and the politics of empowerment.* Boston: Unwin Hyman. Black women's unique ways of knowing, combining feminist, African, and African American roots.

*De Beauvoir, S. (1953). *The second sex.* New York: Knopf. Treatise on the psychological, social, and philosophical bases for women's inequality throughout history.

*Dewey, J. (1956). *The child and the curriculum/The school and society.* Chicago: University of Chicago Press. (Original work published 1902) An accessible introduction to the educational philosophy of the founder of progressivism.

*Finn, C. (1991). *We must take charge*. New York: Free Press. A book-length discussion of the ways our schools must change to focus on academic excellence.

*Friedan, B. (1963). *The feminine mystique*. New York: Norton. A major book that helped launch the modern women's movement by describing "the problem that has no name": women's depression and isolation as 1950s housewives.

*Gilligan, C. (1982). *In a different voice: Psychological theory and women's development*. Cambridge, MA: Harvard University Press. Women's moral development: an ethic of care as opposed to an ethic of justice.

*hooks, b. (1989). *Talking back: Thinking feminist, thinking Black*. Boston: South End. A Black feminist challenges White feminist pedagogical theory.

Martin, J. R. (1985). *Reclaiming a conversation: The ideal of the educated woman*. New Haven, CT: Yale University Press. How western philosophers from Plato to Charlotte Perkins Gilman have constructed women's thought and education.

*Miller, J. (1996). *School for women*. London: Virago. The paradoxes—current, historical, political, philosophical—of educating women and being a female teacher.

Noddings, N. (1992). *The challenge to care in schools*. New York: Teachers College Press. How an ethic of care could transform curricula, pedagogies, and school practices.

*Ravitch, D. (2000). *Left back: A century of failed school reform*. New York: Simon & Schuster. A critique of the progressive education movement that calls for getting back to a traditional curriculum and a common American culture in our schools.

*Spender, D. (1983). *Invisible women: The schooling scandal*. London: Writers and Readers. An early work documenting girls' silences in the classroom and other issues of sexism in education.

Stone, L. (Ed.). (1994). *The education feminism reader*. New York: Routledge. A collection of classic (mostly 1980s) texts on the education of women, including writers such as socialist–feminists Valerie Walkerdine, Madeleine Arnot, and Linda Nicholson as well as Jane Roland Martin and Carol Gilligan.

Taylor, J. M., Gilligan, C., & Sullivan, A. M. (1995). *Between voice and silence: Women and girls, race and relationship*. Cambridge, MA: Harvard University Press.

Woyshner, C., & Gelfond, H. S. (Eds.). (1998). *Minding women: Reshaping the educational realm*. Cambridge, MA: Harvard Educational Review. Reprints from the *Harvard Educational Review* on all aspects of women and education; includes classic articles by Carol Gilligan and Jane Roland Martin and sections on feminist pedagogies, girls and young women, histories, and identities.

Girls, Boys, and Gender Issues in Schools

*American Association of University Women. (1992). *How schools shortchange girls*. Washington, DC: Author. A report based on a national survey about the ways girls suffer discrimination in schools.

Brown, L. M. (1998). *Raising our voices: The politics of girls' anger*. Cambridge, MA: Harvard University Press. Middle school girls in two Maine towns, one working-class and one middle-class, talk about their lives and hopes.

Kenway, J., & Willis, S. (1998). *Answering back: Girls, boys and feminism in schools*. New York: Routledge. How gender reform practices affect teachers, male and female students in a range of Australian schools, rendered through ethnographic accounts. Uses themes of success, knowledge, emotion, and power.

Orenstein, P. (1995). *School girls: Young women, self-esteem and the confidence gap*. New York: Anchor Books. A detailed account of how middle school girls in two schools—White, African American, and Hispanic—face and cope with sexism in school and family settings.

*Sadker, D., & Sadker, M. (1994). *Failing at fairness: How America's schools cheat girls*. New York: Scribners. Popular indictment of sexism in American schooling, documenting discrimination against girls in curriculum, teacher treatment, and school policies.

*Sommers, C. H. (2000). *The war against boys: How misguided feminism is harming our young men*. New York: Simon & Schuster. Argues that feminists have been misleading the public about girls' failures in schools, making girls into victims and ignoring the worse problems that boys face.

Thorne, B. (1993). *Gender play: Girls and boys in school*. New Brunswick, NJ: Rutgers University Press. A noted sociologist of gender looks at patterns of interaction at the elementary school level, exploring the largely segregated worlds of girls and boys.

Walkerdine, V. (1990). *Schoolgirl fictions*. London: Verso. Intersecting with autobiographical musings on becoming a woman teacher, a collection of essays on the construction of femininity in educational settings, how "good girls" and "bad girls" are made, and the costs of the construction of "the child" as male.

Special Education, Tracking Systems, and Educational Inequalities

Harry, B., & Anderson, M. G. (1990). The disproportionate placement of African American males in special education programs: A critique of the process. *Journal of Negro Education, 63*, 602–619.

*Chinn, P. C., & Harris, K. C. (1990). Variables affecting the disproportionate placement of ethnic minority children in special education programs. *Multicultural Leadership, 3*(1), 1–3.

Heward, W. L. & Orlansky, M. D. (1994). *Exceptional children: An introductory survey of special education/Keys to success*. Columbus, OH: Merrill. Textbook that discusses issues involved with special education programs and minority children.

*Kozol, J. (1992). *Savage inequalities: Children in America's schools*. New York: Harper Perennial. Visits to poor Black and rich White school districts expose the severe inequities of school finance across the country.

*Oakes, J. (1985). *Keeping track: How schools structure inequality*. New Haven, CT: Yale University Press. Description and analysis of the causes, conditions, and effects of tracking and ability grouping in our school systems.

*Wheelock, A. (1992). *Crossing the tracks: How "untracking" can save America's schools*. New York: New Press. Shows the costs of tracking and how tracking systems can be undone.

Schools and Racial and Ethnic Diversity

Banks, J. (1988). *Multiethnic education: Theory and practice*. Boston: Allyn & Bacon. A comprehensive introduction to the issues in the field, including resources and practical material for teachers.

*Beauboeuf-Lafontant, T. (1999). A movement against and beyond boundaries: "Politically relevant teaching" among African-American teachers. *Teachers College Record,*

100, 702–723. Using material from segregated Black schools, develops concept of politically relevant teaching, rooted in utilizing knowledge of social inequalities to empower marginalized students.

*Delpit, L. (1995). *Other peoples' children: Cultural conflict in the classroom.* New York: New Press. An African American teacher challenges the student-centered basis of White middle-class progressive education. Working-class and minority children need to explicitly learn the dominant culture's codes as well as their own.

Eitzen, S., & Baca-Zinn, M. (1997). *Social problems.* Boston: Allyn & Bacon. A sociology text emphasizing race, class, and gender issues.

Fine, M., Weis, L., Powell, L. C., & Wong, L. M. (Eds.). (1997). *Off-white: Readings on society, race and culture.* New York: Routledge. A collection of essays on the workings of Whiteness and the assumptions of privilege as the "norm:" how such ideological frameworks shape classroom dialogues and educational settings and what teachers may do.

Ginorio, A., & Huston, M. (2001). *Si, se puede! Yes we can: Latinas in school.* Washington, DC: American Association of University Women Educational Foundation.

hooks, b. (1994). *Teaching to transgress.* New York: Routledge. Lessons on teaching about diversity from noted African American feminist theorist. Essays on multicultural education, Paulo Freire, feminist pedagogies, and other topics.

Leadbetter, B. J. R., & Way, N. (1996). *Urban girls: Resisting stereotypes, creating identities.* New York: New York University Press. Useful and diverse collection of essays on various aspects of the lives of urban adolescents, both girls and boys, of various ethnicities and social classes.

*Liston, D. P., & Zeichner, K. (1996). *Culture and teaching.* Mahwah, NJ: Lawrence Erlbaum Associates. The second volume in this series, which focuses on issues of cultural diversity in school and classroom settings.

Maher, F. A., & Tetreault, M. K. T. (1998). Learning in the dark: How assumptions of Whiteness shape classroom knowledge. In C. Woyshner & H. S. Gelfond (Eds.), *Minding women: Reshaping the educational realm* (pp. 411–438). Cambridge, MA: Harvard Educational Review. How students' construction of gender, class, ethnicity, and race are shaped by unconscious assumptions of Whiteness as the cultural norm.

Martin, J. R. (1985). Becoming educated: A journey of alienation or integration? *Journal of Education, 167,* 871–884. A comparison of women's alienation from androcentric Western education with that of Richard Rodriguez in *Hunger of Memory* as he moves from Spanish to English and from home to the public sphere.

McKintosh, P. (1988). *White privilege and male privilege: A personal account of coming to see correspondences through working in women's studies* (Working Paper No. 189). Wellesley, MA: Wellesley College Center for Research on Women. A groundbreaking essay on all the privileges that White people enjoy because of the color of their skin; widely quoted and used.

*Meier, D. (1995). *The power of their ideas.* Boston: Beacon Press. A noted urban educator and the founder of the Central Park East High School in Harlem shares her ideas about democratic and culturally relevant schooling for all students.

*Moses, R., Kamii, M., Swop, S. M., & Howdud, J. (1989). The Algebra Project: Organizing in the spirit of Ella. *Harvard Educational Review, 59,* 423–443. Description of community-based nationwide project, begun in Cambridge, MA, to teach working-class and minority children algebra in middle school to prepare them for advanced high school classes.

Nieto, S. (1992). *Affirming diversity*. New York: Longman. Biographies, interviews, and ideas about how to create a diverse curriculum, school system, and society.

*Spring, J. (2000). *Deculturalization and the struggle for equality* (3rd ed.). New York: McGraw-Hill. A history of the struggle of people of color for an equal and inclusive education for their children.

Tatum, B. D. (1998). *Why are all the Black kids sitting together in the cafeteria? And other conversations about race*. New York: Basic Books. Essays on the formation of racial identities for children and youth of Black, White, and other ethnic groups. Spells out implications for educators and other concerned adults.

Thompson, A. (1998). Not the color purple: Black feminist lessons for educational caring. *Harvard Educational Review, 68*, 522–554. A critique of the "colorblindness" found in theories of caring in education and psychology.

Ward, J. V. (2000). *The skin we're in: Teaching our children to be emotionally strong, socially smart, and spiritually connected*. Free Press. Based on in-depth interviews with Black parents and teens, Ward explores how parents foster healthy resistance against racism.

Schools and Lesbian and Gay Issues

Epstein, D. (Ed.). (1994). *Challenging lesbian and gay inequalities in education*. Philadelphia: Open University Press. A collection of essays on aspects of being gay and lesbian in educational settings; examples are from the United Kingdom.

Epstein, D., & Johnson, R. (1998). *Schooling sexualities*. Philadelphia: Open University Press. How school settings in the United Kingdom construct sexual identities for teachers and students, enforcing codes of heterosexuality; how gay and lesbian teachers and students cope and construct their own discourses.

Lesbian, gay, bisexual and transgender people in education [Special issue] (1996). *Harvard Educational Review, 66*(2). A broad collection of essays on lives of lesbian and gay students and teachers, both White and of color, in schools and universities. Includes student voices, histories, and curriculum and policy initiatives.

Letts, W. J. IV, & Sears, J. T. (1999). *Queering elementary education: Advancing the dialogue about sexualities and schooling*. Lanham, MD: Rowan and Littlefield Publishers, Inc.

*Lipkin, A. (1996). *Resources for education and counseling faculty*. Project for the Integration of Gay and Lesbian Youth Issues in School Personnel Certification Programs, 210 Longfellow Hall, Harvard Graduate School of Education, Cambridge, MA 02138. Resources for teachers and counselors.

Rensenbrink, C. W. (1996). What difference does it make: The story of a lesbian teacher. *Harvard Educational Review, 66*, 257–270. An in-depth portrait of an "out" lesbian elementary teacher; how she makes diversity work in her class.

Sears, J. (Ed.). (1992). *Sexuality and curriculum: The politics of sexuality education*. New York: Teachers College Press. Essays on the inclusion of gay and lesbian perspectives in the curriculum and the political context surrounding these efforts.

*Stein, N., & Sjostrom, L. (1994). *Flirting or hurting: A teacher's guide on student-to-student sexual harassment in schools*. Washington, DC: National Education Association. Resources and advice for teachers and administrators.

Stein, N. (1999). *Classrooms and courtrooms: Facing sexual harassment in K–12 schools.* New York: Teachers College Press. How school systems throughout the country are dealing with sexual harassment and sexual harassment cases. Useful material for teachers and administrators about how to design and implement policy.

Teaching and Teachers

Biklen, S. (1995). *School work: Gender and the cultural construction of teaching.* New York: Teachers College Press. Examines the experiences of women teachers from many angles: career choice and autonomy, history, and conversations about mothering, community and conflict.

Casey, K. (1993). *I answer with my life: Life histories of women teachers working for social change.* New York: Routledge. In-depth portraits of several female teachers with a social justice orientation.

*Foster, M. (1997). *Black teachers on teaching.* New York: New Press. Black teachers in a variety of settings talk about the challenges of their teaching. Each chapter is devoted to a given teacher.

*Freedman, S. (1990). *Small victories: The real world of a teacher, her students and their high school.* New York: Harper & Row. The story of one demanding and tumultuous year in the life of a New York City high school English teacher.

*Giroux, H. (1998). Interview with Henry Giroux. In C. A. Torres, *Education, power and personal biography: Dialogues with critical educators* (pp. 129–157). New York: Routledge. Interviews with contemporary educational theorists.

Goldstein, L. (1997). *Teaching with love: A feminist approach to early childhood education.* New York: Lang. Based on the work of Carol Gilligan and Nel Noddings, an exploration of the work of two primary grade teachers concerned with the enactment of "loving relationships."

Grumet, M. (1988). *Bitter milk: Women and teaching.* Amherst, MA: University of Massachusetts Press. Examining the lives of teachers in the light of women's experiences as mothers and nurturers. Suggests caring as an antidote to the "categorical and competitive character of schooling."

Hoffman, N. (1981). *Women's "true" profession: Voices from the history of teaching.* New York: Feminist Press and McGraw-Hill. A collection of teacher narratives from the 19th century in both North and South; shows the excitement and challenges of early female teachers' lives.

*Ladson-Billings, G. (1994). *The dreamkeepers: Successful teachers of African American children.* San Francisco: Jossey-Bass. Interviews with eight successful teachers, organized around common themes such as the importance of culture and culturally relevant knowledge, and the roles of family and community.

Maher, F. A., & Tetreault, M. K. T. (2001). *The feminist classroom: Expanded edition.* Boulder, CO: Rowan and Littlefield. Portraits of seventeen feminist college professors in a variety of fields and ranges of higher education instititutions who are teaching about gender, race, and ethnic diversity.

*Rensenbrink, C. (2000). *All in our places.* Boulder, CO: Rowman and Littlefield. Ethnography of three feminist elementary school teachers, showing the wide range of feminist goals, practices, and challenges possible in the elementary setting.

*Rose, M. (1995). *Possible lives: The promise of public education in America*. New York: Houghton Mifflin. The author journeys throughout the country and describes the ways that talented, committed, and successful teachers in many diverse communities work with children of all ages, races, and cultures.

Thompson, A. (1997). Surrogate family values: The refeminization of teaching. *Educational Theory, 47*, 315–339. Discusses the historical and contemporary uses and misuses of the concept of "caring": Women teachers are made to feel responsible for social problems that schools can't solve.

*Weiler, K. (1988). *Women teaching for change: Gender, class and power*. South Hadley, MA: Bergin and Garvey. Interviews and observations of eleven high school feminist teachers and administrators, describing how they became feminists, their goals for teaching, and the dynamics of gender, race, and class diversities in their classrooms.

Feminist and Social Justice Education

*Adams, M., Bell, L., & Griffin, P. (1997). *Teaching for diversity and social justice: A sourcebook*. New York: Routledge. Theoretical and pedagogical frameworks and curriculum designs for social justice courses and approaches, created for the college level but relevant to other levels as well.

*Bigelow, B., Christensen, L., Karp, S., Miner, B., & Peterson, B. (1994). *Rethinking our classrooms: Teaching for equity and justice*. Milwaukee, WI: Rethinking Schools. Lessons and activities for use in the K–12 classroom, including documents, poetry, and videos.

*Grant, C., & Sleeter, C. (1989). *Turning on learning: Five approaches for multicultural teaching*. Columbus, OH: Merril. A series of lesson plans for all subjects and grades incorporating different approaches to multicultural education.

*Levine, D., Lowe, R., Peterson, B., & Tenorio, R. (1995). *Rethinking schools, an agenda for change*. New York: New Press. Essays from the magazine *Rethinking Schools* about curriculum, tracking, and other school policies from a social justice perspective.

*Logan, J. (1993). *Teaching stories*. St. Paul: Minnesota Inclusiveness Program. A veteran successful feminist middle school teacher shows how she works with students to promote gender and other forms of equality and diversity.

*Schniedewind, N., & Davidson, E. (1998). *Open minds to equality: A sourcebook of learning activities to affirm diversity and promote equity* (2nd ed.). Boston: Allyn & Bacon. Activities for elementary, middle school, and high school teachers.

*Wheeler, K. (1993). *How schools can stop shortchanging girls (and boys): Gender equity strategies*. Wellesley, MA: Wellesley Center for Research on Women. Strategies for teachers and administrators inside and outside the classroom.

Journals

Feminist Teacher, Dept. of English, University of Wisconsin, Eau Claire, WI 54702. Articles about feminist theory and feminist pedagogies in the classroom.

Gender and Education, Carfax, 875-81 Massachusetts Avenue, Cambridge, Massachusetts 02139. A British journal focused on sociological studies of gender issues in schooling.

Radical Teacher, P.O. Box 383316, Cambridge, Massachusetts 02238. A socialist–feminist journal on the theory and practice of teaching, emphasizing the college classroom

but with K–12 articles as well. Recent special issues have focused on disability education, working-class studies, media studies.

Rethinking Schools, 1001 East Keefe Avenue, Milwaukee, Wisconsin 53212. A journal for
teachers devoted to issues of race, class, and gender inequalities, particularly in inner-
city schools, and what teachers can do.

INDEX